21 DOORS TO HAPPINESS

Life through travel experiences and meditation

Chit Dubey

ISBN 978-1-9998389-1-1 Paperback

978-1-9998389-2-8 - EPUB

978-1-9998389-7-3 - MOBI (for Kindle version)

SPECIAL THANKS

This book is dedicated to my spiritual master Dr Narayan Dutt Shrimali, who is my true source of inspiration and guiding spiritual force. If he is an ocean, then I am only a drop in it and if he is a tree, then I am only a leaf. He has been a guiding force throughout my life and will be forever, even when I leave my worldly body.

This book is also dedicated to Siddhashram.

CONTENTS

ACKNOWLEDGEMENTS

I would like to thank my father, Shyam Bihari Dubey, who always helped me to aspire to whatever I was looking for in life. I also thank my mother, Annpurna Devi, for her continuous support and to my brother, Sanjay Dubey, and sisters Reema Dubey and Kiran Dubey who always stood by me during difficult times.

I would also like to thank Kevin Boylan and Sara Donaldson, who edited and proofread this book with the focus and critical thinking that shaped it in the right direction.

Many thanks to Indian spiritual and social reformer, Mayank Gandhi, and to conscious electronic music artist, Nathassia Devine.

Special thanks to my friends: Kalicharan Bisht, Frank C. Dauenhauer, Anne van den Berg, Raquel Girones, Tia Lena, Mo, Marina Lepp, Tomas Martinez Buero, Dom Cave and Karolina Paulina Paluch who encouraged me and gave me the feedback I needed. I am thankful to God that I am blessed with good friends and family.

Also special thanks to all my meditation students. They all have been very kind.

This book is illustrated by many real incidents and situations, wherein I met strangers who later on became my friends. I would like to say thanks to all of them for enriching my life experience.

My love and gratitude also goes out to everyone else who knowingly or unknowingly helped me in writing this book.

INTRODUCTION

Have you ever wondered why, in this modern world, everyone is running after wealth, a career, relationships, power and fame, in the hope that they will discover inner peace in the process – but somehow this never seems to happen?

Human beings have become more restless and resentful than ever before. The discomfort of our souls is growing each day and our minds are becoming more impatient. But if we dive deep inside ourselves and search for the reasons behind this, we find that no one is focusing on peace. Our priority in life is never to find peace, though we always complain about its absence in our life.

I have always had an urge to probe the questions about human existence that come to my mind. Through this book I want to share the answers that I found through my own experiences, walking on the face of this earth and observing the world around me.

My objective is to make you stop for a few moments, to think about which direction you are heading in and for what purpose, and to help you enjoy this journey

in a peaceful manner. I believe that we should attain
wisdom and become more aware in our day-to-day
lives, and while doing so, contribute towards a better
world and try to make this world free from greed,
discrimination, wars, and violence.

Each chapter of the book covers a different aspect
of life and ends with a practical exercise (or sutra),
the goal being to find a balance between your inner
and outer worlds. These exercises are offered to you
as examples of my deep meditation.

The simple meaning of meditation is to 'be in the
moment and be aware' and there are many ways to
attain this. Each chapter is going to provide you with
a tool to help you be in the moment. There are many
books written on meditation, by many masters, often
teaching different techniques; everyone is trying to
help you achieve awareness and live in the moment.
Through my own experiences – spending time at different ashrams and observing the harmony there – I
have come up with a few simple techniques that will
help you to find inner peace and to retain balance in
the outer world. They are simple, and are suitable
for anybody.

Each chapter will help you to experience freedom in the truest sense and get rid of anxieties: to
become a free-spirited soul and finally reach the state
of 'happiness'. This book will help free you from much
negativity – your expectations of life, the burden of
pursuing wealth and the sense of being in the 'rat race';
the stress that can accompany relationships; feelings
of anger or jealousy and indeed the conditioning of

society and religion. After practising all the exercises (sutras) you will be in tune with your heart and soul.

My humble request to my readers is to keep practising each chapter's sutras many times, throughout your life. No matter how short or long each chapter and exercise looks, surely and slowly it will help you to achieve your final goal – peace, freedom and love.

Each chapter is divided into two parts. The first part is about one specific topic and the second part is one exercise (sutra) to practise. You can read the contents of this book in any order according to your preference. You can move back and forth based on your choice. If possible, please practise exercises which you liked continually for 21 days to yield better results.

Shantih is a Sanskrit word which means 'peace', and Sutra means 'thread or string'.

Therefore, please find yourself some time in your busy life to go through each page and move towards peace, freedom and love.

With much Love

Chit

THE MUNDANE WORLD

$\cdots$ [1] $\cdots$

A GOAL IN LIFE

Take up one idea. Make that one idea your life – think of it, dream of it, live on that idea. Let the brain, muscles, nerves, every part of your body be full of that idea, and just leave every other idea alone. This is the way to success.

Swami Vivekananda

There is a famous story about a poor man (Dashrath Man-jhi) from Bihar, India, who carved a 110 metre long road through the Gehlour hills, working day and night for 22 years from 1960 to 1982. His feat reduced the distance between the two Gaya districts from 70 km to 7 km.

Though initially mocked for his efforts, this only served to strengthen his resolve. But as time went by, and the unfazed farmer continued to split the troublesome hill in half, he started getting some help. 'Though most villagers taunted me at first, there were quite a few who lent me support later by giving me food and helping me buy my tools', he remembered. Now all the people of Gaya city have nothing but gratitude for the 'Mountain Man' who made their lives so much easier. This ordinary man became extraordinary and inspired many of his villagers and also others across the country, just by doing something for society with a goal in mind and through practising perseverance. Not many people realised his achievements while he was alive, but without looking for attention he kept doing what he believed needed to be done.

When I read about this man and his life it inspires me and makes me realise how important it is to keep taking small steps towards our goal each day. Unless we maintain progress everyday with conviction, we will never be able to achieve what we aspire to do in life. This poor man kept doing what he believed he should have been doing, and in this way made travelling easier for thousands of people and inspired millions throughout India.

For every human it is important to find a goal in life, for otherwise it is so easy to get lost. One can easily get distracted from one's journey and each day we will find hundreds of excuses for not doing what we always wanted to do. We will find every possibility to waste our time and keep complaining that we do not have any time to fulfil our dreams.

When I see successful people in this world, I always wonder what their one special attribute is that makes them stand out? And I always get only one answer: their passion and focused approach for their work and goal. They seek to attain their goal every day, and to turn it into reality. That is the only difference between the common person and a successful person. The common person first of all is scared to dream, and if they dream, they only do so in their imagination, and never put much effort into transforming the dreams into reality. But a successful human lives with that dream – breathes that dream every moment and puts every effort into making it a reality. I have always believed that once we have decided to do something, nothing can stop us. If anything stops us, it is just our negative thought processes and lethargic lifestyles. The negative thoughts that arise in our minds kill positive thoughts. Unfortunately, most of the time it is the negative thoughts that win and they drive life in the wrong direction. We all fall prey to negative thoughts. But life moves quickly, and so if today I look back to my childhood and reflect on my journey to the present day, I might realise that time has passed so quickly and still I am not able to do things that I wanted to do with my life.

Most people take time for granted. They think that there is infinite time and it is never going to end. They live in an unplanned way and they do not realise this until they reach old age, and by then it is too late. And some people do not even realise this in their old age! They only realise it when death is near, and for some people this realisation never even happens. Once you become aware of the passage of time, the question becomes: are we only born to eat, sleep, have family, earn money, grow old and die? Or there is something more to life?

So it is important in life to have a goal, to chart out a plan and to stick to it. Create a goal and live each day to achieve that. And if possible, create a small goal for each day and try to achieve it on daily basis. Our future is nothing but a continuing sequence of days, each lived fully. Or as Abraham Lincoln said, **'The best thing about the future is that it comes one day at a time.'**

There are millions of people who are lost in our mundane world, and they keep living for the false dream of tomorrow, and tomorrow never comes. Their happiness disappears in the waiting, and then when finally death arrives they feel cheated.

They keep thinking, when I have enough of a bank balance I will do these things; when I achieve this position in my career I will pursue these goals; or when my kids have grown up, I will definitely accomplish these objectives, but this idea of having 'free time to work on my own goal' never happens. It never happened in the past for any human, and it is not going to happen for you. Life is NOW – it is always now or never. If you do not desire enough, or if your intentions are not strong enough, and if your actions are not in the right direction for the things you aim to achieve then they will never happen, no matter how many millions you save, no matter at what age your kids are, and no matter if you become an owner of a company; these things you really want to do are still not going to happen. Time is not waiting for you: it is moving at its own pace, and time is limited for every individual. You came onto this planet with limited time (death is inevitable), and you have to leave one day, and even if you do not want it, nature is going to push you on – it happened to countless billions in the past, and the same will happen to everyone in future.

Time is constantly moving, no matter how slow your actions are – for every individual existence is moving slowly towards death, and you have to be organised to achieve the things that you always wanted to do. There is no second opportunity in your present life to finish your work, so you should believe that this is your first and last birth and that you have to finish everything within a single life. If possible, when you decide on a goal write it down, then keep looking at it before going to sleep and once again when you wake up in the morning. This list of actions to do will fill your heart with energy and you will observe your actions starting to move in the right direction. Your life will take a big turn and you will experience the joy and bliss of accomplishment and self-contentment. Only real actions are going to give you happiness, and only real actions are going to make you successful in your endeavours – desires and empty goals are not enough to push your boat out. You should first learn to paddle before you sail in an ocean, then the entire ocean will become available, but through your paddling you have to give direction to your boat; in same way you have to keep trying in life to keep your direction. The world is enormous and you are not going to achieve everything you want, so you have to be specific and particular about your objective, and start moving your actions towards that. When there are no distractions left, then things will start to happen as we imagine, dream and perform our actions.

Therefore if today you have a dream, create enough passion to make that dream reality. Start working from this moment, and start living each moment before it is too late and the time you once had has gone.

For example, right now if you desire to have a coffee – you will go to the kitchen, boil the water, put some coffee in a pot or mug, add the water and your coffee will be ready. Only the desire of having the coffee was not enough, so you needed to put your actions behind that and it happened. It is the smallest example I am giving you. In the same way, if you want to be a dancer, a writer, an artist, an athlete, a teacher or a social worker, nobody is stopping you from becoming that – all you need to do is to put your energy and actions behind achieving this goal.

And please do not create a goal just to get attention, because the desire should always be towards attaining the happiness within your soul, and only your actions are going to give you this. To expect love and affection from others is a secondary element – it is not the true nature of a soul, it is an illusion and you should avoid it. Real happiness is found by working towards a goal, and not in enjoying the adulation of people. Your goal should be towards satisfaction of your soul and it hardly matters how others see it.

No matter how small your goal looks to others, your focus should be to fulfil your life by doing the things that you always wanted to do. Every human being is unique and you are also unique among billions of people living on this earth, and so are your dreams and your journey.

Every moment is very precious and if we look back, starting from our childhood to the present moment, the one thing that always remained constant was our dreams. No one will deny that they do not dream, and everyone dreams to do something good in life, but only a few are able to fulfil this. And you never know whether your personal goal might touch the lives of millions around the world in the way a poor man from a village in Bihar province inspired millions in India.

I implemented these changes first in my own life by writing a few lines every day so that I would be able to finish this book one day. I was not anxious about how many people would read it or like it, but my focus was to keep writing and to share my experiences about the world. Let us see whether my words stand up through the test of time. Maybe one day my readers will decide this.

As I explained in the introduction, each chapter is going to introduce one simple technique of meditation that will help you to live a more focused and peaceful life. If you have now finished reading the first chapter, then please practise the following exercise. I have named each exercise Shantih Sutra, which means 'Peace Thread, or the Principles of Peace' in Sanskrit

SHANTIH SUTRA 1

Breathe In and Out

Breathing in and out is the most essential part of life but it is so ordinary that we take it for granted. If we breathe in and out with complete awareness and a focused mind we can avoid many problems in life: and that is why each chapter gives a high importance to breathing technique. I request that you practise all these exercises with complete awareness. Just like you breathe in and out every minute, in the same way you should practise all these exercises many times in your life. In the beginning it might be difficult, but once you start practising and experiencing a positive change in life, you will enjoy it more. Please do not give up early on, for it takes time to get used to it. Let's start with the first practice outlined below.

Breathe in and out 10 times with closed eyes.

When you take a breath – make it long and deep, hold it for a second, and then release it slowly. When you breathe in, fill your lungs with fresh air and then empty them completely while breathing out. Repeat this 10 times with complete dedication and there should be no excuse for not doing this.

Preferably practise this while sitting in a relaxing position, but if you cannot find any place to sit at the moment and are outside your home, you can practise there as well. You can practise while sitting in an office, while standing in a metro or bus, or while sitting in a park. It will only take a few minutes and you will feel much better and more relaxed. If your mind is full of anxiety, anger or worries – this practice will bring instant relief. It will also help you to make sensible and meaningful decisions in your life.

I would appreciate it if you practise this technique since it is a first exercise and it will also show your commitment to yourself.

· · · [2] · · ·

THE POWER OF THOUGHTS

*All action results from thought, so it is
thoughts that matter.*

Sathya Sai Baba

It so happened that a Zen master was lying on his death-bed, surrounded by hundreds of his disciples. Everyone was waiting for him to say something and to pass on his last message before leaving, but he was silent. After a few hours his closest and oldest student asked him, 'Master, before you leave this body, please share your last words of wisdom', and with a struggle the master replied, 'Unlearn all that you have learned so far. Forget the wisdom I told you and discover your own truth. Consider that everything I taught you was a story. Go in search of your own truth and develop your own authentic thought processes.'

You should be very careful about what you are thinking, as there is every possibility that life will present you with exactly that. Watch the thoughts that you allow to enter your mind, because these thoughts will send invitations to the outside world and then things start to happen.

While I was travelling in Belgium, I decided to visit Barcelona, but I had no idea what I would do there. I had not planned anything and the tickets were not even booked, but nonetheless I started thinking about Barcelona. I was walking around a museum in the beautiful city of Bruges, when suddenly a couple asked me to take their picture. After taking their picture I asked them, 'Where do you come from?' and she replied, 'We are from Barcelona.' I smiled and said, 'I am planning to visit your city. I am excited and I am going there for the first time. I have not booked my tickets yet.' Then this girl and her boyfriend started telling me about the nice places to visit in Barcelona.

They gave me a lot of advice about things to do in this city.

We spent an hour together, talking and discussing lots of things. They drew a map of Barcelona on a piece of paper with the places to visit, and then explained to me what I must see, where I could stay and what precautions I should keep in mind, etc. They also invited me to join them at a music festival they were heading to.

Later I observed that my thoughts about Barcelona also attracted other people from the same city. I find that this universal law works for me, and I think it works for everyone. Many people might dismiss it as just a coincidence, but it is not: there were hundreds of people roaming around that museum at that given time. I have experienced such things many times in my life – it is magical. Your thoughts attract the same kind of people, so be careful and watchful about what you think. All types of uninvited thoughts knock at your door, but you have to choose which ones you allow in or not.

The same thing happened to me in Paris. It was my last night in Paris and the next morning I was travelling to Rome. After a long day of touring this city I was accompanying my friend to the metro station. He was my friend from Paris whom I had met in Dar-Es-Salaam, and when he got to know that I was visiting his city he had kindly found enough time for me and spent four days showing me around. When we were crossing the street, we decided to have our last drink together. We were sitting outside a bar with our bottles of beer when suddenly a woman came to me and asked, 'Why are you sitting here alone? Why not join us?' She was part of a big group. 'Where do you come from?' she asked. 'From India', I replied. She seemed happy to hear this and said, 'Really? I've been to India 12 times. I love Indians, it's a great country.' She then introduced us to her other friends who were from Italy, Turkey and Morocco. They were lively people and invited us to join them.

They were sitting at a nearby table and a few minutes later I was dancing with a woman to Latin American music. She tried to teach me a few steps of the tango but I was struggling to copy her. When I mentioned that I know the basics of salsa, however, she asked her friend to select some salsa music on the jukebox and then we danced salsa together. Once the dance was over, I asked her where she came from, and she said she was from a small town close to Rome. Out of nowhere I had found people in the street, and we ended up having a nice conversation and a lot of fun together, but most importantly this lady was from near Rome in Italy, which was going to be my next destination

After that I accompanied Francki to the metro station, and when I returned to my hotel I went straight to the internet café. There in the cyber café I met four young guys and all were from Italy – two of them were from Rome. When I told them that next morning I was flying to Rome, they were happy to hear this and they gave me few tips about places to visit

Because the journey to Rome was in my mind in Paris, I found that there I met people who would assist this. So as I said, be careful about what you think, for successful people in this world think positively and therefore life becomes positive for them.

For example, while people can commit suicide from the top of a mountain, alternatively painters can paint beautiful paintings from there. Or a person might hang himself from a tree, but perhaps later on a poet can write a great poem about the same tree. Life is all about the reflection of your positive or negative thoughts and how you see life.

Put simply, positive thoughts will make your life positive and negative thoughts will make it negative. Though it is true that in certain circumstances it becomes extremely difficult to think or remain positive, but again, the negative approach cannot help us in such situations – the only thing that could rescue us is to be motivated from inside and to allow positive thoughts to override negative ones and transform things around us. This world is a projection of your thoughts and you have the power to filter or direct your thoughts. It is like your house – if someone knocks at your door and you do not want to allow them inside, then you will not open the door, or after a brief conversation you will close it. Your mind is also like this, so you must be responsible for what you think and what kinds of thoughts you permit to dominate your mind and heart.

SHANTIH SUTRA 2

Breathe In and Out

Breathe in and out 30 times with closed eyes.

The above technique must be practised in a sitting position only. Sit with crossed legs on the floor or sit on a chair in a relaxed position with your back straight. If you do not have the right place to practise at the moment, then wait until the time when you do. It is important to practise this technique with dedication and a focused approach.

· · · [3] · · ·

DESIRE, ACTION AND PATIENCE

You have a right to perform your prescribed duty, but you are not entitled to the fruits of action. Never consider yourself the cause of the results of your activities, and never be attached to not doing your duty.

Sri Krishna

I was in Barcelona and went to see the world famous Camp Nou Football Stadium. When I reached there I found that on the following day the opening match for the season 2013–2014 between Barcelona and Levante would be played, and it was an opportunity for me to see my favourite football player. This news made me happy and my next action was to buy tickets. But soon I found that I was too late, and someone told me it was not possible to get tickets for the next day's match because the tickets were already sold. I also asked an official at the ticket counter but he replied, 'Sorry, the ticket counter is closed now.'

However, I decided to sit next to the ticket office. I don't know why, but I thought let's sit here and see. I was in Barcelona as a tourist for only five days. So it's not as if I could have planned to see the next match, and for me that was my last opportunity because I was soon travelling back to India and was not sure if I would return to Spain again. I was sitting there and looking at the ticket office with the hope that maybe they would somehow open again (though this was not practical). After an hour of waiting at the bar opposite that hope disappeared and at last I was enjoying the moment, just sitting, drinking beer and looking at the people passing by – the sun was about to set and it was getting darker.

Later on a young guy approached me and asked, 'Are you looking for tickets? I have one extra ticket.' This guy was like a spring of water in a desert. He had no idea how happy I was in that moment, and I instantly replied, 'Sure, why not? For how much?' But I was a little bit worried as to whether it was an original or not, so I asked him, 'Sorry, but is it an official ticket?' and he replied, 'Don't worry, it's an original. You see, I bought a more expensive ticket later on and now I want to sell the other. You can trust me. It's official.' Finally, I bought the ticket and got in to see the match. The young guy I met was from Oman and he was studying in Barcelona.

That day I found that dreams, action, and patience truly bring fulfilment in life. No matter how small my dream was in that moment, on that day had I not waited, I would never have got a ticket. Instead, I experienced that action and patience can bring unexpected events that mean something in life. Many times in my life it happened that whenever I showed patience after performing actions I received better results – the fruit of action and the patience that follows becomes what we call 'luck'. The way a farmer ploughs the field, sows the seeds and then waits with patience for the harvest-time to come, in the same manner action and patience must be combined. The way a farmer cannot control the weather, you also cannot control the outcome.

I would like to share another story here – in Mumbai I met a Vietnamese girl at a social gathering and at that time she was only 19 years old. When I asked her what she was doing in India, she replied, 'I'm travelling, and thinking I might travel for another two years around the world.' I thought that she must be rich to travel around the world, and I asked her how she financed her travel. She replied, 'I'm not rich, I just want to keep travelling and I'll do small jobs to earn me enough money for survival. While doing this I plan to write a book, for I want to be a writer or a journalist.' This idea sounded to me like a big dream that required a lot of daring. I recalled that when I was 19 I did not have enough courage to follow such an extreme path, but here she was, already doing that. How many of us at such a young age desire to do something like this? It is hard to meet such people. I wished her good luck on her journey and told her, 'Let me know when you get published. Let's stay in touch.' So we exchanged each other's Facebook IDs and stayed in touch.

After a year I received a job offer to work in Dar-Es-Salaam and when I posted this on Facebook, that I was travelling to Tanzania, to my surprise this girl commented on my post that she was living in Dar-Es-Salaam at the time. We exchanged contact numbers and decided to meet there. When I arrived in Tanzania she was the first person I contacted, and it was a pleasure to see her after such a long gap. At that time she was travelling in East Africa. She told me all her stories of wandering in Africa and it was lovely to hear about those adventures.

She had worked in bars, restaurants, casinos, and also did baby-sitting to help cover her expenses. At that moment she was staying for free with an American family, and she was in a bit of a panic about what she would do once this American family left Tanzania. She also told me that she now felt a little bit tired after so much travelling, and that she would like to go back home and finish her book. She said that her book was already half-finished and that every day she tried to write something.

After a few months I saw her post on Facebook to say that her book had been published and was selling well among readers. This crazy girl had achieved her dream by following the principles of passion and commitment. When I met her the first time two years back, many people would not have taken her desire to be a writer seriously, but she was very much convinced: and she achieved it. This girl is a true inspiration – no matter how little a dream is, we first require a strong desire that leads on to action, and then finally we need patience to accomplish it. There is no other way to achieve a goal.

If we read stories of successful people we find that they all had strong desires, faced many obstacles and challenges as they carried out their actions, waited patiently for the results, and finally they succeeded. They fulfilled their desires and now we all listen to them or read about them, and they are our daily inspiration. Therefore why are we stopping ourselves from achieving our dreams?

Having a dream and then following it with complete passion are two different things. If you want to be a dancer, a writer, or a film-maker, but do not want to follow this path because the results are uncertain and do not guarantee the fixed income of a routine job, then there is every chance that you might end up at the end of your life with dreams and desires unfulfilled.

No normal human would take the step of putting their stable life at risk to try different things. No normal human would like to go beyond their safe cocoon and experience the big and crazy world out there. But I met people in Africa who were cycling across the entire continent, an old couple (80 years+) in Nairobi who were travelling in a caravan and camping at random places they found in Africa, and a teenage Vietnamese girl who travelled alone in India, Asian countries, and the African continent, and who later became a writer.

If you do such things you will be considered crazy, but there is no harm in being labelled as crazy and following an unusual path that career–family oriented people would like to avoid. But if you know that this is what you want to do and it brings happiness to you, then the world's opinions become irrelevant. Throughout history, many explorers have travelled alone and discovered new countries and civilisations during their journeys. They were passionate about their dreams and helped millions who came after them. People like Aristotle, Martin Luther, Charles Darwin, or Albert Einstein were so convinced by their dreams that they did not care for the rest of the world, and the result is that the entire world admires them.

Mahatma Buddha is one of the best examples – he renounced all luxuries, his wife and his family, and wandered in search of the truth. That was definitely not the right path for the majority at the time, to abandon everything and go in search of truth, but the legacy he left behind is immense. He inspired billions of people. His thoughts are still alive after 2,000 years and are going to be here for many centuries to come.

So keep carrying out your actions, no matter how big or small they look in the moment – we should always be convinced by our goal to achieve it. If we do so, then life becomes easier and the universal energy supports us in achieving our objective. And sometimes it also happens that while chasing our dream we discover ourselves and realise that we, in fact, want something else completely and not the dream we are chasing at the moment. But such realisation will never happen unless we work on our dreams with commitment and passion.

When I quit my job at the end of 2009, I wandered for two years around the Indian film industry to become an actor – and in the end I realised that I did not want to be an actor; I wanted to be a writer. But during those two years of trying, I discovered myself.

Life passes quickly and it is easy to get lost. Maybe by the time you are thinking to start working on your goal, your youth has already gone and you cannot travel back in the past. Yet most people who achieved extraordinary things were involved for a long time with their thoughts and initially the public was not ready to accept them or their ideas, but gradually as they reached their peak, people started to appreciate their wisdom. This is how the world is – the revolutionary leaders were always alone in the beginning and it was only at a later stage, or in many cases posthumously, that people discovered them.

Helen Keller is a great inspiration, for despite her physical disabilities she wrote great books and inspired millions throughout the world. If anything is stopping us from achieving, it is always our lack of action and lack of commitment towards our goal. If we have a goal and we are not working towards it, this means we are only daydreaming, and unless our dreams are making us restless, we are not going to achieve anything.

I am not saying that your goals should always be revolutionary and aimed towards changing the world. You could have any goal: a good education, a career, travelling, having a family, helping society, scientific or spiritual journeys, etc.

But every desire requires action, planning and direction, otherwise we will be lost on our path. It will not take much time to grow from teenage to middle-age, and then from middle-age to being an old person, and then one day we all have to leave this world. So we need to be more focused, and should plan our actions accordingly.

Only strong desires lead to action, and once the action is done we still require patience. Therefore do not be disappointed if things do not look positive at the moment or if you are tired of waiting for something to happen – if you do your action and practise patience, you will find the direction in your life.

The combination of desire, action and patience has worked for many, and it will work for you as well.

SHANTIH SUTRA 3

Breathe In and Out

Now, you have to do the same meditative exercise that you did in the previous chapters 50 times. Do exactly what you did in the second chapter, but this time the breathing in and out must happen with a minute's pause in-between:

Breathe in and out 25 times with closed eyes, and then take a pause for one minute.

Next breathe in and out another 25 times with closed eyes, and then take a pause for one minute. If you would like to repeat both stages multiple times, please feel free to continue and keep repeating until you are comfortable.

The above technique must be practised in a sitting position only. If you do not have the right place to practise at the moment, then wait until a time when you do.

It is important to practise this technique with dedication and a focused approach.

··· [4] ···

RELATIONSHIPS

The most painful thing is losing yourself in the process of loving someone too much, and forgetting that you are special too.

Ernest Hemingway

Once I met a German girl who was staying in a meditation ashram in India for three months. I saw her always busy doing many different courses, and one day out of curiosity I asked her, 'What are you looking for? I see you're doing almost all the courses and also the most expensive ones. Did you find what you were looking for?' and she replied, 'I had a bad break-up. I was in a serious relationship for five years and once it was over I was destroyed. So now I want to forget my ex-boyfriend, but he is still stuck in my mind.'

In life, a great many problems are due to either relationships or money. Those who are single want to be in a relationship, while the ones who are in a relationship are looking for a reason to get out of it. It is hard to find people who live together for a long time and who are still madly in love. There are such people, but their numbers are few.

Like the human mind, our relationships are a complex subject to understand. We experience millions of thoughts in a day, and in the same way there are millions of ways to see a relationship. It exists at various levels and always takes a new dimension based on the circumstances and on the person you are in a relationship with.

Before trying to understand relationships, most importantly we should try to understand ourselves, our true nature, this life, its meaning and its purpose. And the first step is to start falling in love with ourselves, as only then will we be able to see love outside. If we fail to understand our own true nature, then how can we understand someone who is completely external to us? We need to put effort into finding peace and love within our own hearts, and only then will love have an opportunity to bloom for us in the world outside.

Broadly, relationships exist at two levels: material and spiritual. To attain a materialistic relationship is easy – it is based on the physical level, around sexual desires and greed. It happens quickly, and fades in the same fashion. Those who only come together in search of solely physical relationships quickly get bored, and they either end up separating or they decide to spend their entire life with the same person, but with regret. They never really love each other, but being too scared of dying alone, or from other insecurities, they decide to live together for the rest of their lives.

External energies are not in our control, and the other person's behaviour is not within our sphere. The other can never be controlled by us but, sadly, this is what we try to do in each relationship. No one is ready to accept the other the way they are. We all have expectations before we enter a relationship, and then at a later stage the relationship becomes an ego clash that results in a battle of possession. The moment someone tries to possess the other, their love dies. The problem begins when we forget to appreciate the other person for the way they are.

We should accept others in the way we accept ourselves. Every human is unique and has a different personality and no matter how hard someone tries, they still cannot become like somebody else – that is why love and true relationships should begin at an individual level. Firstly your mind should connect with your own soul – unless this happens, the entire journey will be futile and you will be disappointed by each attempt. Once we can achieve this successfully, then we can begin to understand others.

The friction in relationships happens when we like someone and start expecting them to return the favour. But life is not like this, it does not promise you will get something in return just because you desire. Many people fall in love, spend time together, and after some time the spark disappears, emotions disappear, and they start looking for a new relationship. In many cases they go into depression, cling to the past, suffer, and in some cases they require medical help or need to visit spiritual ashrams (meditation communes) to restore their balance in life.

It is important to find a proper balance when two people are together. If you are materialistic and your partner is spiritual then it is not going to work out, for there will always be arguments because you are at a completely different level and your purpose in life is different. So it is important to find similar kinds of energies and then grow together. If you are materialistic, you will find more harmony with a person who is also materialistic. In the same manner a spiritual person will be much more comfortable with another spiritual person – the energies should be aligned in any relationship.

Relationships should be a process where two souls are ready to learn from each other. And such a relationship is not going to happen unless the ego dies. We cannot keep destroying our true identity just to satisfy our partner's ego, and even if we do so, in this process our ego will remain alive forever.

Unless you can experience the free flow of energy between two souls, where without uttering a word your other half understands your feelings, things will not improve much.

Every soul has a male and a female energy and is in search of its opposite energy in the other person. But instead of diving deep inside first, we start looking outside.

If you are a female and go deeper you will experience your male energy, and the same law applies to a male. Even if you want to stay single, you can achieve the energy of a relationship alone, and the simple way is to start loving yourself, recognising your own feelings and appreciating your own journey – but while practising this you should be careful, or you could be easily deceived by your own ego.

The day you start to understand yourself, you will start understanding others as well. And the day you find someone who is also ready to accept you the way you are, you will experience harmony in a relationship.

The easiest way to overcome your negative experiences is to go into yourself deeper through meditation. Then you do not need someone else to experience happiness. And once you start experiencing inner happiness, and become more spiritually aware, you will be able to see relationships in a more positive way.

I will use a commonplace analogy to explain a relationship – imagine you are sitting in a plane from London to Berlin and you start a conversation with a fellow passenger. You provide enough space for both of you and listen to each other throughout the journey, and when you arrive at your destination you go off in different directions. But if the conversation was nice, maybe you will try to keep in touch in the future and share contact details. Or if the conversation was not so good and you could not establish any kind of bonding, then you just forget that person without any ill feeling or sadness.

In relationships too, we need to respect each other by providing each other with enough space, and at the same time understand that we met because we had a common goal in the same time frame, but it might be possible that after a few weeks, months or even years we realise that our goals are now different, and although in the past we spent a beautiful time together, now it is time to move apart without holding any grudges.

In simple words, a relationship is when you can relate with someone – this someone could be an external or internal energy – and the timeframe could also vary, sometimes across months or years, or perhaps even a lifetime and sometimes many lives.

SHANTIH SUTRA 4

Breathe In and Out

Now you should work a little more, so you have to do more breathing in and out. But remember it is just a beginning and we have to move slowly towards our final goal. The most important thing is, while doing this exercise your stomach must be empty – so it is better to do it in the morning or, otherwise, there must be a gap of at least three hours after a meal before practising the exercise below. Even after a glass of juice, you should wait for one hour before practising. Make sure your stomach is empty and that the food has completely digested before starting this exercise, and the eyes must also remain closed throughout.

Breathe in and out 30 times with closed eyes, and then sit silently for one minute.

Breathe in and out 30 times with closed eyes, and then sit silently for two minutes.

Breathe in and out 30 times with closed eyes, and then sit silently for three minutes.

Throughout the entire process please keep your eyes closed and you should be sitting somewhere on the floor, on the ground or a flat surface to feel comfortable. While sitting, your back must be straight but the rest of your body should be in a relaxed position. You should not become stiff, so you should sit up straight with your arms resting on your knees.

If you are feeling sick and cannot sit, you can do this while lying on the bed. Follow the same instructions – but if you are too ill then do not practise it; please respect your body and make your decision based on your body's energy. If your body does not allow you, then simply avoid this exercise and practise later when you feel more energetic.

· · · [5] · · ·

GREED AND SUFFERING

The ignorant mind, with its infinite
afflictions, passions and evils, is rooted in
the three poisons: greed, anger, and delusion.

Bodhidharma

It was my second day in London and, after enjoying the view from the London Eye, I was walking towards Westminster Bridge. At the bridge I saw some people were gathered and were watching something. Out of sheer curiosity I joined them. Soon I observed that one guy was sitting in the middle playing a trick, and everyone was gambling on that. A Spanish man was hiding a small ball under three steel cups and after a few shuffles here and there, asked people to guess under which cup the ball was hiding. And when people pointed to the right cup, they earned double the money that they had bet. Many people were betting and a few of them were earning.

The game intrigued me, and now I was taking more interest as I couldn't stop myself from participating: but I didn't want to spend money. I was able to guess under which cup the ball was hiding and I was right every time, and many people who won had taken my advice. At this point I was asked by the guy who was running the game to put some money down, or otherwise he wouldn't allow me to keep predicting. This time I decided to put up money as I felt very confident with my experience, so I bet £20. But the man refused to allow me to gamble 'only' £20, and everyone around persuaded me to put more money down so I could win more. In the end, I was encouraged to bet £60. But when he lifted that small steel cup there was nothing underneath – I was shocked and had lost £60.

I had no idea what went wrong because before this whenever I had pointed my finger I was correct, but this time when I put my own money in, it went wrong. I was sad but still kept watching that game in the hope that something would happen. So I stood there for another 15–20 minutes and was observing the game minutely, and once again I *got involved in playing. Somehow I had to get back my lost money. I thought I would get my money back by playing a few games because I saw some people were still winning there, so why not me? I made a decision to play with £30, but everyone there was telling me, 'No, put more, you are right, the ball is there. We are a thousand times sure.' An Arab guy who was standing next to me said 'I could put £500, but unfortunately I do not have it.' A woman standing next to me bet £100 and I was inspired enough to bet £60 again. But when he lifted that cup, again there was nothing underneath. Now I was completely devastated. I had no money left in my pocket; I had lost all £120 in cash that I was carrying for that day.*

Later, cops came along and everyone dispersed. Those who were running the show were clearing up quickly and speaking among each other in Spanish. Now I had no idea what to do and how to get back to my hotel on Oxford Street. I had no money left and was not carrying my credit card. I was angry with myself and also realised that I had fallen into the trap simply because of my greed. Those guys had cheated me cleverly and I had been easily fooled. But I was still responsible for this.

Later, a few people who saw me losing money came to me and said that I should not have played that game, at least not with such a big amount. They told me that those tricksters were part of a big group and that the ones who were winning were part of the same group – a very well-planned trap for foolish tourists like me. But the damage was already done and as life never gives you a second chance, I took this as a lesson learned and decided to never repeat such a mistake in the future.

With a grumpy face and feeling like a loser, I started walking towards Parliament House. When I checked my pocket I found a few small coins – all put together they came to 91 pence. I was feeling hungry and thirsty, but that money was not enough to buy anything in London – it is one of the most expensive cities in the world. Even the bus ticket to my hotel was at least £2–3. It was still my second day in London and I was not aware of how the streets connected. Everything was new to me. I reached Trafalgar Square and as it happened, collided into the Pride Parade which was on that day. So I spent some time there watching the parade to try and change my mood, and later on I asked some policemen for directions. So after two hours of walking, I finally reached my hotel. I will never forget that day and the way I fell into the trap of my own greed. And there is another incident that I would like to share:

It was my first week in Dar-Es-Salaam, and I was returning to our hotel with a couple of colleagues from Paraguay. My friend from Pakistan, Ashfak, was in the front with the driver, and the rest of us were in the back. It must have been around 3 pm, and we were all sweating as the air conditioning inside the car was not working. We had opened our windows, but still, the heat was unbearable. Then all of a sudden we saw a big military truck, which overtook us and stopped in front. It was an open truck, and there were dozens of soldiers standing in the back, staring at us. Most were holding guns, and were dressed in a green uniform, with hats and boots. And a few were murmuring together, and pointing fingers at us.

With his path blocked, our driver got scared and braked. We all looked at each other. Two guys who looked liked officers jumped out of the truck and marched towards our car. Their uniforms were drenched, and sweat was pouring from their faces.

'We're in trouble', our Tanzanian driver whispered. So we all waited anxiously for what would happen next.

'Get out of the car ...' one of the officers shouted.

'But what's our fault?' the driver asked.

'It's a one-way road. Come out, and give me the car keys.'

The driver handed them the car keys, and for a while they argued in Swahili.

'Sir, could you please speak English?' I asked.

'Why should I speak in English?' replied the officer. 'You should speak Swahili. You are in my country. You come out now, and I'll teach you my language.'

My question had infuriated him. Ashfak and I left the car and started talking to them.

'Sir, every day in the morning we go down this road, but it's always been a two-way lane until now ...' Ashfak said.

The officer shook his head. 'No,' he said, 'because today it was changed to a one-lane road. You can't argue with us. Go to prison or pay the penalty!'

Ashfak stared at me for few seconds and then sighed, 'Ok, how much is the penalty?'

'How much do you have?' grinned the officer. This

question led to a different conversation and, after bargaining, we had to pay US$200. This event gave all of us a bad experience, especially the two colleagues from Paraguay who were there only for a short business visit. This opportunistic greed reflected badly on the country the soldiers were supposedly defending.

These incidents are just small examples, but we humans inflict untold devastation on ourselves and others for the sake of greed, all the way on up to waging wars and destroying societies.

We are mostly greedy for money, power, fame, or sexual desire. We might be greedy enough to expand our religion or political or economic structure across the entire world and in the process inflict mass destruction on everyone – greed has many forms. But in whichever form greed takes, it only leads to great suffering.

SHANTIH SUTRA 5

Silent Meditation

Now we have to go deeper. We should work a little more and have to do more breathing in and out, followed by a new exercise. But remember that it is just a beginning and we have to move slowly towards our final goal. The most important thing is, while doing this exercise your stomach must be empty – so it is better to do it in the morning or, otherwise, there must be a gap of at least three hours after a meal before practising the exercise below. Even after a glass of juice, you should wait for one hour before practising. Make sure your stomach is empty and that the food has completely digested before starting this exercise, and the eyes must remain closed throughout.

First stage
Breathe in and out 30 times with closed eyes, and then sit silently for one minute.

Breathe in and out 30 times with closed eyes, and then sit silently for two minutes.

Breathe in and out 30 times with closed eyes, and then sit silently for three minutes and then proceed to the next stage.

Throughout the entire process please keep your eyes closed, and you should be sitting somewhere on the floor, on the ground, or on a flat surface to feel comfortable. While sitting, your back must be straight, but the rest of your body should be in a relaxed position. You should not become stiff, so you should sit up straight with your arms resting on your knees.

If you are feeling sick and cannot sit, you can do this while lying on the bed. Follow the same instructions – but if you are too ill then do not practise it; please respect your body and make your decision based on your body's energy. If your body does not allow you, then simply avoid this exercise and practise later when you feel more energetic.

Second stage: 10 minutes
Close your eyes and let all kinds of thoughts enter your head. Keep them flowing as they happen in the moment, but this time you have to watch them from far away. Watch all your thoughts like you watch a movie or look at a painting. Keep watching your

thoughts but just do not be a part of them. You only have to be a witness to your thoughts. If your thoughts make you smile, smile, and if they make you sad, become sad, and after watching the game of your mind for 10 minutes, try to stop your mind from thinking. Try to focus on the spot between your two eyes and become focused on nothing else.

Third stage: 10 minutes

For the next 10 minutes you should close the doors of your mind to thoughts that enter, but do not struggle and waste too much energy if your mind is still wandering and thoughts are flowing. You have to be aware with your thoughts.

The focus change to complete silence will not happen suddenly – your habits are your oldest friends and they will not leave you so easily, but with time and practice they will realise that you are no longer interested in them and they will start leaving you alone. After 10 minutes, open your eyes and the exercise is finished.

This technique should be practised every day, and you will see positive changes in your thought process and life if you practise it continuously for at least 21 days.

Please do not get disappointed if your mind wanders too much while sitting silently. It takes months or even years to reach the stage from where you can experience complete silence. With time you will learn the art of observing and experiencing the silence between thoughts. Think of it the way you do years of continuous study to become an engineer, teacher or a doctor – it is only then you become a qualified professional. In the same manner, to control your mind, you need full concentration and constant work to become a master of it. Otherwise, you will be a slave of your mind throughout your life. Therefore, please do not surrender and keep practising no matter how much time you get to do this. Each day and passing year you will keep improving and observe positive changes in your lifestyle and behaviour. This practice works on your mind and soul in a subtle way, and only by practising it for a long period will you be able to see the changes in your life. But once this happens, it will be an everlasting change that shapes your ideas and the way you see the world around you. You will be more in tune with yourself – mind, body and soul.

· · · [6] · · ·

A ROLE MODEL

Be the change you want to see.

Mahatma Gandhi

I was 10 years old and living in Jabalpur, Madhya Pradesh (a central state in India). It's a small city in the central part of India and my father had been posted there by the Indian army. One evening, my mother gave me money and asked me to go and buy eggs from a grocery store. I went alone to buy eggs but when I reached there, the shop owner by mistake gave me 12 eggs instead of 6. The shop was crowded and he thought that I had paid for a full dozen. I felt pleased with myself and thought, 'Today I will have a few extra eggs to eat' and returned home. When I got home and my mother saw the extra eggs she asked, 'How come you have extra eggs? I didn't give you that much money.' And so I proudly explained the entire story to her. But my father overheard this conversation and he immediately scolded me and said, 'Go back right now and return those extra eggs. I didn't teach you to lie and steal things, and you should never try to run off with anything that you didn't earn.'

So my happiness quickly turned into a nightmare, and I soon returned the eggs. That was the first practical lesson in honesty taught to me by my father and today, when I look back, I say thanks to this honest and humble man. In that moment maybe I was miffed with my father's severity, but now I feel grateful to him. Some lessons in life you do not appreciate the moment they occur, maybe because you are not mature enough to see it or to relate to its overall purpose. But after a few weeks, months or years you realise that those incidents happened for a reason.

And here is the message – to be a role model you do not always need to be an Abraham Lincoln or a Mahatma Gandhi. If you aim for this, there is nothing better, but even living in an ordinary way you could be a role model for the people around you. In the case I have described, my father was the best example to me. And the first step towards being a real role model is to be honest in whatever you are doing in the present moment. You could be a great parent, a responsible citizen, a good employee, or an honest neighbour or friend. If my father had encouraged me in that moment for my cheating, I could have become a scoundrel later on in my life; his encouragement could have led me onto the wrong path and maybe I would have become a cheat or a chancer. But instead of praising me, my father scolded me and asked me to return those eggs. By teaching me these simple principles, he became my role model. Although his neighbours might not have been aware of his strength of character because he is a shy person, he became my hero and influenced me in positive ways.

During my college days I observed a few students who were always busy helping classmates to solve their university assignments or trying to reinterpret complex formulas so that their peers were better able to understand. They always put in extra effort after the regular classes to teach their classmates, and this helped them to pass their exams. Of course human beings are not all born with equal talents, but everyone is gifted with something special. A few people are good with maths, a few are good with literature, and a few do well in sports. Simply through sharing your ideas and skills with others, we create a positive society. I always recognised that people who were helping others were not looking for rewards, but instead they found happiness by sharing their knowledge. Such people in turn become role models among their circles of peers or friends.

We can in the same way be a role model for the people with whom we spend our time every day. If we start observing the people around us, we can see our role models. The only thing is that we never notice them as we are too busy looking for role models that are too distant from us.

By practising a few simple principles of honesty, a disciplined life, and by helping others, we could be the guiding force for some of our fellow human beings. If we could help even a single person move in the right direction, then that would be a great service to humankind. The whole point of existence is to go beyond our own selfish desires and to help others. Without needing exposure on TV or in the newspapers, we can become role models for other people and experience the happiness that it brings for ourselves.

SHANTIH SUTRA 6

Read Books & Listen to People of Wisdom

First stage
Breathe in and out 50 times with closed eyes, and then sit silently for two minutes.

Breathe in and out 50 times with closed eyes, and then proceed to the next stage.

Second stage
Sit silently with closed eyes for 10 minutes, and then proceed to the next stage.

Third stage

Today you either have to choose a book to read that teaches about life, or listen to some person who has great wisdom.

As Franz Kafka said: **'A book must be the axe for the frozen sea within us.'**

Reading books always helped me to understand myself and this world better. The best thing about books is that a few people poured their entire wisdom into a few pages. And when you read a book, you get everything in a few days if it is understood well, but the authors have spent their entire lives gaining this knowledge. So for readers, discovering their wisdom and experience of life in just a few pages is the easiest way to learn.

A few people are extraordinarily gifted in certain areas of life. If you read the biographies of some successful people, you will observe that from the age of five or six they were doing activities that even at the age of 70 we will not be able to. It shows that such people were so gifted that they were further ahead than the rest of the human race. They often spent their entire life in one particular field, hence it is important to listen to such people, at least as long as it takes for them to pass on their knowledge on that particular subject.

Mahatma Buddha spent his entire life in meditation and exploring the intricacies of life. Mahatma Gandhi devoted his life to practising non-violence, truth and honesty, and he brought about a revolution through his ideas. If we want to learn about meditation, we should listen to Buddha or to Zen masters, since they spent their entire life researching this one subject. They are more learned, and there is a lot for us to learn from their wisdom. If someone wants to practise meditation, it is better to go and practise the teachings and the path that is already been shown to us instead of going and discovering a new wheel for the same purpose. But again, at the same time it is important that you do not become rigid and fanatic while following the path, as it might be that you can discover a better or different way at a later stage once you know the basics.

As Mahatma Buddha famously said,

'Don't blindly believe what I say. Do not believe me because others convince you of my words. Do not believe anything you see, read, or hear from others, whether of authority, religious teachers or texts. Do not rely on logic alone, nor speculation. Do not infer or be deceived by appearances. Do not give up your authority and follow blindly the will of others. This way will only lead to delusion. Find out for yourself what is truth, what is real. Discover that there are virtuous things and there are non-virtuous things. Once you have discovered for yourself, give up the bad and embrace the good.'

In same way, Gandhi's book, The Story of My Experiments with Truth, gives you a detailed tale of how this man survived with just truth and honesty, and even though there were conflicts at many stages, he tested himself and proved his method right. MK Gandhi's books and wisdom will help you to also practise truth, through the ways that he used.

In the same way, Albert Einstein researched about

matter and his theory of relativity, so it makes sense to read his works if you are interested in this subject.

But sometimes our ego stops us from listening to someone or reading someone's words. The ego says, 'Why should I follow and listen to someone?' But in life, it is better to learn and adopt ideas that have already been developed by others and this way we can move quickly along in human evolution, and invest our energy in discovering something new that has never been explored.

For example, if a girl goes to nursery school, she needs to listen to her teacher. She needs to learn the alphabet, so there is no need to re-invent the entire alphabet on her own. She just needs to show faith in her teachers and to learn the basics, and down the line after a few years when she finds her own way, she could invent new things and in turn gift these on to this world.

I always make sure that I read the books of successful people from different fields, listen to public speakers, and likewise listen to motivational speakers and learn from them. Every time I listen to them, I learn something and it helps me. In today's world there is enough information that is available for free, so the only need is to have the desire to learn and then put in some effort.

Reading books of wisdom is going to change your perspective on life. Some people explored their inner worlds deeply, and they shared their wisdom through books. These pages too are going to enrich you for sure.

· · · [7] · · ·

TRAVEL IS THE BEST TEACHER

What you seek is seeking you.

Jalaluddin Rumi

A man was imprisoned since birth and spent his entire life behind the prison walls. He never had an opportunity to see anything beyond them. He had no idea how beautiful the world was outside. He had only heard stories about the ocean, the sun, the moon, trees, mountains and children. As he was completely ignorant of the outside world, he created his own world within those four walls. He painted the walls of his cell entirely with pictures based on his imagination and the stories he heard from people who had seen the world and lived outside the prison. But one day those walls fell down, and for the first time in his life this prisoner was a free man. For the first time in his life he saw a blue ocean, a shining sun and dancing moon, trees full of fruits and tall mountains, which he experienced with the innocence of a child, and then realised that where he was living all those years with only his imagination as a guide was far from the reality.

As a teenager when I used to see backpackers in Delhi, I used to wonder why they were travelling around with such big and heavy bags. Was it fun to travel all alone, leaving everything behind? At that age I could not understand the fun and meaning behind it, so I used to watch them while I was sitting inside the school bus and looking out of the window, when they were standing at the roadside. What were they looking for and what was the reason behind this? This question always intrigued me, and in the end it inspired me to start travelling myself. Over time I learned many things about this activity and I decided I would experience it only by travelling far from my birthplace and country. Finally, when I took my first job and became financially independent, I decided to travel. First I travelled within India, but later on I went further afield to other nations.

My job gave me the opportunity to work in the USA, Africa and Europe, and I seized it. I travelled further by taking sabbaticals from the job and used this to explore the world. But now the question I asked myself was what had happened to me through my travels? Did I find anything? Had I explored something that no one else could, or, was I still in the same dilemma about travelling as when I was a teenager?

The answer was positive – I explored many things during my years of travelling that I will have to write down in a separate book, but I will also try to write a few lines in this chapter to allow me to do it some justice.

By travelling, I had discovered myself and also the world. Travelling broke me out of my limited world and conservative home space – it showed me that there are people who think with a different approach towards life, and you can learn from them. In India, from childhood, we are taught that ours is the best country, and I believe every country must be teaching its citizens the same ethos. There is a famous saying in the Hindi language that says 'Mera Bharat Mahaan'. This means 'My India is Great'. Of course there is no harm in saying this if you have only lived within India and have not travelled anywhere else. For then obviously there is nothing to compare it with. But once you start travelling and observe other social systems and political structures, you realise that your country needs to learn many things from other places.

It is then that you start to question this phrase 'Mera Bharat Mahaan'. Such a saying merely brandishes a myopic ego, and false pride is not going to make any nation better. The same principle, of course, applies to every country on this earth; there is lot that we can learn from each other. Every nation teaches its countrymen to believe that they are the best, and the way they do things or see things is the only way. I see a strong political motive here – unless you fill people with 'national pride' then they will not feel much of an attachment to their country, and if this continues then the concept of the nation state might soon become obsolete.

Unless people felt great about their nation it would be difficult for them to die in its name, and for wars we need people who are ready to die 'in defence of the national territory'. But you soon start breaking out of such preconceived notions once you start to travel and you find that the entire world is your home. It is then that you start to ponder the famous words written in the Vedas, 'Vasudev Kutumbakam', which mean 'the entire world is a single family'. So the same thing happened to me. Through my travels across the US, Africa, Europe and Asia, I learned many new things and evolved as a human being.

Another example – before travelling to the USA I had certain perceptions about the country that I had observed through television programmes, movies and magazines. I had this perception that people living there must mostly be rich and living as equals with an easy-going life. At the same time I used to think that they must be arrogant and less friendly to someone coming from India or Asia. But when I started to work in Atlanta with a big French IT consultancy, I learned many new things about this country in three months. I broke free from my prejudices and saw that the USA was not the same place I had imagined before. Instead I saw people from widely mixed backgrounds: Africans, Latin Americans, Europeans and Asians who had all been living there for many generations. I discovered that America was in fact very much a multicultural and integrated society.

At weekends I used to take a taxi to visit downtown. My driver was an American and he used to share his experiences of life in the USA. He told me once, 'most white Americans are friendly to people who are from a different place of origin in America, and they treat everyone equally, except for a few cases of racism, but then this happens everywhere and we should definitely minimise such incidents.' He said that he preferred Indians as customers, because they were doing well paid jobs in IT companies and did not mind paying him the right money. He considered these Indians intelligent and highly qualified. It was an eye-opener for me that for some Americans India was not necessarily a poor country. In the past I had met a few Americans who had told me that for them India was poor, hot and corrupt, but now I had finally met someone who had a positive outlook towards my country.

The same taxi driver also mentioned that he loved the great spiritual philosopher and writer Rabindra Nath Tagore, and that his life changed after reading his books. He had visited India a couple of times in the 1970s and he could recite lines of Tagore's famous book Gitanjali very well; that I found impressive. He was inspired by the spiritual wisdom of India, and he shared with me an experience he had had while meditating in Rishikesh, in the Himalaya Mountains. His outlook towards life had completely changed after spending just a few months in India, but finally he had to come back because of his family and work in USA.

Then there was another taxi driver, an African American, whose parents had originally moved to the USA from Nigeria. He used to drop me at the office in the morning, and sometimes I also used his service to go to the city centre. While talking, he told me that he charged more money from white people and less from Asians or Africans. When I asked the reason behind this, he told me he did not like white people because he still felt oppressed and discriminated against in the US every day. He had a deep anger inside him and he was quite biased against white Americans. I did not believe his story, however, because the same country would later elect a president who was of African origin and this president was not elected once, but twice. So this taxi driver's generalisation of white American society was completely wrong. It might be possible that he had met with some prejudice and racism in his life, but it does not mean that the entirety of white American society is against black people.

My interaction with these two taxi drivers, who had such different attitudes to life, made me realise that the fight is not between the white and black or brown races – the fight is always between the ego and ignorance. Religion, nations and skin colours are just tools to be used: there is always human greed and violence behind it. Human greed, violence and the ego is at the core of what is wrong with the world and they use nations, religions and races as a tool to achieve their objective. For example, the first taxi driver had a positive outlook about his country, India and the world. He was a well-travelled man and was not biased against anyone. This was because he had travelled outside his country and had put in effort to learn and to see good things. But at the same time that he was talking about the many good things in American society, he was also able to highlight its negative elements.

But the other taxi driver who was also American and born and brought up there had a revulsion against his fellow countrymen, and that is why he was not able to see the positive things in life. His outlook was limited and with the way he was seeing his country, his behaviour was reflecting this – like charging more money from white people, etc.

The USA gave birth to great leaders, like Abraham Lincoln who fought for black freedom. He was a white American and the president of America, but he became the leader who abolished human slavery in the USA. For this he suffered and was finally assassinated, hence there is no reason to label the entire country as racist.

I have had many similar types of experiences when I was travelling in France, England, the Netherlands, Spain, Russia and other European countries. I found people who had different opinions about the society in which they were born, and I saw stark differences in their social behaviour based on that.

Another example could be my travel to the UK as an Indian, there to unlearn and learn. India was a British colony for more than 200 years and as Indians we always read in our school books about the atrocities inflicted by the British Raj, and because of this there is still hostility among many Indians towards the British government. But when I arrived in Britain for work and lived there for a while, I realised that most British people appreciate their Indian community and many also accept the mistakes of the past. The younger generation has nothing in common with the dark past of colonialism – whatever happened in the past is over and we need to see how we can live peacefully in the present and create a stronger bond between us for future generations.

I remember one incident in Madrid when I was attending an international gathering organised by a leading social media group. There I met a businessman from Belgium. He was the first man I spoke to once I entered the club. When he introduced himself and told me he came from Belgium I said, 'Belgium, that is a great country.' He immediately replied, 'No, I believe that India is a great country, not Belgium'. I was shocked at his reply and asked, 'Why do you say so?' He continued, 'I have been to many countries around the world on business, and also because I love travelling. India has given a lot to the world. Its knowledge, ancient wisdom and message of peace is revolutionary and has revolutionised so many world leaders around the world.' He paused little bit, smiled and then again said, 'I know that, being a Belgian, it does not sound good to say that India is better than

Belgium, but I do not believe in national boundaries. I do not feel proud about what my country did to the Congo in the past and especially King Leopold II, and you do not become great by selling beers and chocolates.' I was awestruck by his blunt reply. 'What do you want to drink?' he asked. 'Let me buy the first round,' I said to him, 'you can buy the second.' During our discussion he revealed that he had been much influenced by Indian spiritual wisdom. Although he was aware that India still had to work hard to eradicate poverty, caste-based discrimination, poor living conditions and corruption, he still saw it as a great and inspiring country.

While travelling around the world and after having long and deep conversations with my fellow human beings, I have realised that we cannot expect a utopian world on this earth – there will always be social problems and injustice. But we can also see that wherever compassion and love is stronger and more prevalent in society, there will be more peace on earth. We need more human beings to be filled with love and compassion, and that is the only way to make this world a better place to live.

Our world will always be visited by great figures like Krishna, Buddha and Christ. They will sacrifice their entire lives to teach honesty and truth and to set an example of love and compassion. We will also keep seeing social leaders like Abraham Lincoln, Mahatma Gandhi, or Nelson Mandela who will give us the hope that no matter how adverse our circumstances are, we can create harmony in this world. If we can truly accept and recognise such visionaries and if more people come forward to support them, then this world will be a more peaceful and beautiful place to live in.

We should not live with a false hope that one day there will be no wars, famine, drought or injustice in this world. Sadly, injustice will be there in the future as well, but the ratio between justice and injustice can vary – based on how many human beings are trying to make this world better and more peaceful. This key realisation only happened to me through my travelling.

SHANTIH SUTRA 7

The Courage to Accept Your Mistakes

First stage
Breathe in and out 50 times with closed eyes, and then proceed to the next stage.

Second stage: 10 minutes
Close your eyes and let all kinds of thoughts enter your head. Keep them flowing as they happen in the moment, but this time you have to watch them from far away. Watch all your thoughts like you watch a movie or look at a painting. Keep watching your thoughts but just do not be a part of it. You only have to be a witness to your thoughts. If your thoughts

make you smile, smile, and if they make you sad, become sad, and after watching the game of your mind for 10 minutes, try to stop your mind from thinking. Try to focus on the spot between your two eyes and become focused on nothing else.

Third stage: 10 minutes
For the next 10 minutes you should close the doors of your mind to any thoughts that enter, but do not struggle and waste too much energy if your mind is still wandering and thoughts are flowing.

After this, with closed eyes try to remember who you cheated or hurt the most in your entire life. Just ask, from your soul, to whom you are causing the most suffering. Today you have to call that person and apologise sincerely. Today you have to leave aside your ego and pride and find a way to communicate to that person, and if possible, to meet with them personally and express your feelings of regret and repentance.

This exercise is important. If you cannot do it now, I request that you come back when you have enough courage to do this exercise but please do it. Today you have to clean your heart and move ahead in life. You have to leave your past, and the burden you are carrying in your heart, behind. Remember – your journey is not the first or the last, and if you cannot move away from this feeling of guilt, you might continue to suffer on until death and maybe afterwards as well.

No matter if you cheated someone in a friendship, a relationship or a business deal, or hurt them through any means, today you must find the time and courage to apologise, confess, and unburden your soul.

In life we keep too many burdens in our hearts and suffer all the time because of them, but it is not required. The moment we accept responsibility and throw such feelings out, things start moving in a positive direction again and life brings us new opportunities.

SECTION 2

THE SOCIAL WORLD

· · · [8] · · ·

SUCCESS AND HAPPINESS

Try not to become a man of success, but
rather try to become a man of value.

Albert Einstein

I was travelling through a small city in Pushkar, Rajasthan, India, and when I entered a restaurant for lunch, I observed a young man with a serene face looking at me. After taking a chair in the opposite corner I looked at him again, and saw that the famous book, Autobiography of a Yogi by Param-hansa Yogananda was lying on his table. The man looked thin, he had a beard and tanned skin, and I could see from his complexion that he was from a Western country. Soon we made eye contact with each other and then he broke the silence with the Indian greeting, 'Namaste'. I greeted him likewise and we entered into conversation.

The man was an American in his thirties and he used to run a tech company. He was doing pretty well with his business and was considered successful by his peers, but at the same time he felt that a lot was missing from his life. Although he was a wealthy man, he was not happy about the way his life was unfolding. He mentioned that in the beginning chasing wealth was what he wanted to do, but later on he realised that this was no longer true. One day he asked himself, 'Is this what success in life really means?' and he became restless, lost interest in his business and started looking for answers elsewhere. He told me that he couldn't sleep properly during this period and he was terrified by the vision of the rest of his life following the same pattern, feeling empty and unfulfilled in his heart. There was an existential struggle being waged inside him and in the end that changed everything.

During his teenage years he had read a lot on philosophy and spirituality, and once again he returned to those books of wisdom to find answers. In the next few months he started wrapping up his business, and later he sold his company. When he made the decision to stop doing business, all his *friends and family criticised him and called him a 'loser'. So the man was rejected by the same people who had previously been admiring him, and overnight his 'success' was now labelled as a 'failure'. After selling his business he decided to travel and visited India, and at that time he was living in a hermitage on a mountain. This small city in Pushkar is surrounded by many mountains and is quite popular among Western tourists, so it's quite easy to meet 'hippies' there. When he was telling me all this, I was so fascinated by his story that I forgot that my food was already served and I no longer felt hungry. The man's face was glowing; no one could miss his deep smile and calmness. I found his conversation enriching and inspiring.*

Success and failure are subjective in life. For many, a successful life means amassing wealth, becoming famous, or holding power and being in a position to command people. Ironically, the meaning of success in this world is based on how many people know you and how much wealth you have. Our 'success' is measured on the criteria of how many times we appear on the front page of a tabloid or how many interviews we give to news channels. Success has been so commercialised that it has lost all meaning and led people to crave this type of false lifestyle.

Celebrity culture has been promoted by the media and people crave to become part of this elite club. There is also so much hype around materialistic possessions that people will go to any length to achieve this. No matter whether it is in business, art, politics etc., 'success' means competing in the same rat race. The public appreciates you for your glamour, awards, fame, power and glitzy lifestyle. Most people are in awe of money and glamour and they ignore the fact that many people sell their souls, compromise their principles, and trample on truth and justice to attain all this.

Instead of success being driven by inner happiness and peace, you are encouraged to be dependent on the recognition of others.

In reality, the true meaning of success can vary for different people, based on their perception of life. If we define it in simple words, it means: if you are able to do the things you wanted to do and live life peacefully without compromising on human values, you should consider yourself successful. If you live life peacefully and also help others in achieving peace and happiness, then likewise you should be considered as a successful person. If you can hold your head high when you look back on the past and your soul takes pride that you followed your inner path regardless, you should feel successful in life irrespective of fame or wealth.

When I was involved in the Indian film industry, I saw first-hand how much compromise people inflict upon their principles to achieve fame in show business. To maintain their facade of glamour they opt for debt, spending more than they earn. Instead of being happy from the inside, they pretend to be happy on the outside. They compromise on their artistic values to get a minor role in a big TV soap or a movie. They put their entire lives at stake just to chase the illusion of increasing fame. They do not want to be actors because they enjoy the art of acting or the theatre; they just want to be part of the media system because they love the stardom, glamour and the wealth it brings – the essence of art drops off the agenda completely and the only thing left is business. Such people consider themselves successful if they appear on TV or in newsprint, but otherwise they live in depression. They hire full-time paid PR agents who work for them to ensure that they keep appearing in newspapers or magazines and on TV. They borrow money to buy the most expensive clothes and to rent the most expensive flats, but usually they do not earn enough to afford it. This entire process kills their happiness from inside, but somehow they are sucked so far into this sham success that it becomes difficult to move away from it. Show business becomes their virtual reality and real life gets put on hold. Such a disconnected dual life brings too much pressure, and some become mentally ill or even commit suicide. This type of obsession is, of course, not only limited to the film industry, but also to other fields.

I saw young kids who had run away from their families or left college and had arrived in Mumbai in search of fame – and their goal was to make it big in Bollywood. There is no harm of course in chasing your dream, but your dream should have depth and meaning. Your dream should not be to 'become famous and rich'. Your dream should be towards finding happiness and discovering yourself. If your dream is to go in search of truth, art, creativity, invention, and happiness, then it makes sense if you rebel and in this way you may help your society as well. But unfortunately we live in a world where success means adulation and a consumerist lifestyle, and this is promoted through powerful conduits.

In the true sense of the word, successful people are those who devote their lives to empower poor people, women, street kids, the disabled etc. and try to bring a change in society. Successful people are the ones working for human rights, the environment, or against corruption and discrimination, or who are trying to bring justice to this world. Successful people are also those spreading awareness or those trying to teach something new and meaningful to help the present and future generations. But shamefully we do not see much point in praising them, and they are often neglected.

So, to be a successful person, we do not need to amass an excess of wealth and power. By living an ordinary life, but with honesty and simplicity, we can live a successful life. For example, if as parents we live a peaceful and honest life, then we can impart these values to our children. After all, our kids are going to be adults tomorrow and in this way they can become better citizens. In the same manner, as community doctors or school teachers we can work relentlessly in our professions and contribute enormously to our society.

Success also means that you follow the direction that you always wanted to, no matter how much people may discourage you.

Once I was attending a writing workshop at the annual Kala Ghoda Literature Festival in Mumbai, which is world famous. At the end of the workshop we were given some assignments and we all had to write a piece of work within a given time frame on a given subject. After 15 minutes everyone was going to read aloud their work and then the judges were going to announce their verdict. The subject was 'How does a prostitute looking for work interact with the brothel owner for the first time?' We were advised to write up the conversation between this pair of imaginary characters in a creative manner. But when the time came and I read my work aloud, the judge immediately requested that I stop reading my write-up.

She attacked me in front of everybody and shouted loudly 'You should never try to write, and drop this idea of becoming a writer – get back to your routine job.' I have to admit that at that moment I felt humiliated and dejected. But later on I found the strength to dismiss her judgement, because it was just her opinion and other peoples' insults should not affect me or my life's journey.

So I carried on following my passion and I never stopped writing, for if I had taken that woman's judgement to heart on that day then I would have failed completely. I told myself not to be damaged by her derogatory pronouncements, and I carried on with my work. Success is not bought easily: it has to be struggled for with hard work. This means to keep doing what you believe in, regardless. For me, writing is the best way to express myself and to share my observations of life. It is a meditative and cathartic process through which I find inner peace. Just because someone once criticised me in a publicly humiliating and disrespectful manner, I should not discourage myself. Instead of giving me her critical feedback (which I would have readily taken on board) she tried to destroy my dream, and we should never allow anyone to kill our dreams. Dreams are the soul of life and they keep us going against all adversaries – and to fight until the end to achieve this, that is what constitutes real success.

Our goal should be to resemble the flower that blossoms not to please others, the sun that shines when it has to, the birds that sing not because someone is listening, and the peacocks that dance to express their joy and happiness. If we are able to live our lives simply and freely like them, we are successful.

When I was teaching meditation every weekend in Dar-Es-Salaam, Tanzania, sometimes I had very few students and I was not able to cover the rent of the studio, and sometimes I gave free classes. Regarding this, a few friends questioned why I should spend money from my own pocket to teach others. But the process of sharing knowledge and teaching made me happy inside, and I kept on conducting those work-shops because I had found happiness through sharing.

As I said in the beginning, we should not crave to do something with the notion that in return people will appreciate it, but instead we should do it because we really enjoy it and through this we can find our inner happiness. And the day we find that happiness inside, no one in this world will dare to put a price on it. Happiness is precious and must be preserved at any cost, for no matter how many obstacles appear along the way, this sacrosanct space must always be protected.

Inner happiness is the most important element

you need in order to live a successful life, and it can only occur when we do not put a price on our soul. And if we achieve happiness from inside, then we are successful in life.

SHANTIH SUTRA 8

Revisiting Happiness

First stage
Breathe in and out 50 times with closed eyes, and then proceed to the second stage.

Second stage: 15 minutes
Sit silently with closed eyes for 15 minutes, and then proceed to the third stage.

Third stage: 30 minutes
Close your eyes and revisit the happiest time of your life. In the present you have to once again relive each moment that happened in the past. You have to watch

these moments second by second like you are play-ing a video and the control is in your hand. You now have to relive this happy time again and again with closed eyes. Those happy moments will again make you happy, and this happiness will build positive energy inside you. It will bring a smile to your face, and through it you will acquire a positive approach to life.

This will seem transitory, but it will work if you do it for 30 minutes every day over a month. These 30 minutes will take you into the past where you were happy, and you want to live that kind of life now. This happiness will teach you that the happiness of the past can be created and lived in the present moment as well. It will also teach you that the past moment is over, and you now have to live a life that should be as happy as the past used to be. Sometimes your mind is stuck at the happiest time of your life and it is never able to move out of the past, because you keep comparing it to the present every day. Hence, it is important to relive that past consciously again and with awareness, and to slowly let it to disappear from mind so that you can come back and create a magical moment in your present and future life.

WEALTH AND SHARING

No one has ever become poor by giving.

Anne Frank

Once, the disciples of Buddha brought a poor and starving man to his ashram and asked him to teach the man words of wisdom. Of this, Buddha replied that the poor man required food more than words of wisdom, so his disciples should feed him first.

Poverty should not be tolerated by any society and we must try our best to eradicate it. If we are living in poverty, we will not be able to understand the deeper meaning of life. If someone thinks that by going through such suffering they will understand this world better, then it is not going to happen. If you are wealthy, then there are more possibilities for you to help the world and understand it on a deeper level. But being rich does not mean you should have a stingy heart. It is important to have a generous heart to share with others. It is important to keep a fine balance between the materialistic and spiritual life. You should be paid enough to live a decent life. You should be able to wear good clothes, live in a nice house and provide quality of life for your family members, but your entire life should not be based around it. You should not end up just chasing money, because it is a never-ending process and you will never be satisfied.

Money can solve many problems in life and it can empower you to help others in the world. If you had enough wealth, for example, then theoretically you could help many poor and impoverished people to rise up out of disease and poverty. Your money might alternatively create better schools, hospitals and orphanage centres. Your money could bring light to the lives of thousands of children. But charity must also be spent wisely, and you do not have to give away all your money. Instead you must discern how your money can best be utilised for a true purpose.

Unfortunately, you do not often see many rich people being charitable. There are only a few with millions who come forward and start giving back to this world that gave them so much. But if you think for a few minutes, you realise that you were born naked and everything you earned in this world occurs only after your birth. When you leave it you won't be able to take it with you, so why not share with others? There is a 'logical' argument in capitalist thinking that asks why someone should share their wealth after so much 'hard work' to achieve it, as this concept of labour is understood. To answer this I would like to take an example of a tree.

As a tree grows, its shadow falls on an ever-wider area of ground under its leaves. The tree protects this piece of land from the sun and the rain, but it also provides protection to human beings and animals when they look for shelter. The behaviour of the tree remains the same for all. Because it is rooted to the land, it does not discriminate against others. When the tree grows and becomes stronger, it remains essentially detached from the land it sits on and never does any favours intentionally to any individual. It treats everyone equally and no one is closer to or farther from it.

Just like a tree, every human being should try to practise the law of detachment. When we are born into this world, we arrive through the union of two people we call mother and father. When we grow older and become wiser, it makes sense to give back to them and also to our own future family, but it should not restrict us from also sharing with others. If we grow materially, socially and spiritually, then the first shadow will fall on our family, but whenever someone comes to us for help then we should treat them in the same way.

Whenever the moment of judgement comes to take the right decision, we should never consider who is close to or far from us. All human beings should be treated equally, and our decision must only be based on the principle of truth, love and compassion for all.

Sharing makes us more human, because although materialistic pleasures have no limit they are also limited. After earning millions, you will chase after billions. If today you are the richest person in your country, then tomorrow you would like to become the richest man in this world and so it goes on, incessantly. There can only be one richest person in a single country or in the world. And once you reach this level nothing much changes, but you have to struggle to maintain your position, and if you descend to the second position you become dissatisfied and once again you spend your life trying to get back to the first position. You will keep on doing this unless you say to yourself after a certain point, 'that is enough for myself, now it is time for others.' This way you will help and inspire many, and maybe a few might follow in your footsteps. This chain of charity will keep multiplying until we create a better and more equal world on this earth.

But if everyone focuses instead on accumulating

individual or class wealth, then we will only see ine-
quality and a huge disparity between people, and this
is prevalent in today's world.

In many countries, only 1% of people are con-
trolling more than 75% of the wealth and this is
insane. Whenever only a few individuals control all
the wealth, the rest will obviously fall into poverty
because resources are limited in each region.

To bring equality we do not always need a big
political revolution followed by some new order that
is going to change the world, because after such revolutions we often find ourselves confronted by new
rulers who start doing same thing. We only need to
create better opportunities for everyone, and such a
culture is created only through the principle of sharing
our common humanity.

We should encourage people to share on their own
initiative and beyond limiting the extremes of ine-
quality we should not enforce this primarily through
law, but through education. We need to create a world
where solidarity is part of daily life.

Of course it is not easy to practise what I have
said above. The attachment to money is so strong
that it becomes almost impossible to start sharing
with others. Somehow, the entire society is so built
around money, that even the thought of sharing it
starts to look foolish.

In fact, in order to share, you do not need to have
much wealth, and the forms of sharing (knowledge,
etc.) can be different. For example, when I was part of
an international hosting community, I hosted dozens
of people from all over the world in my small and

modest room in Mumbai – and at that time I was jobless and not earning a single penny. I was restless and pretty busy, but I still found time to host those travellers. I never felt ashamed about how these people would feel when they arrived at my ordinary room, or how they would react to that. I just did it. I was renting a flat that was given by the Maharashtra regional government to poor people, of a type of residence called SRA (Slum Rehabilitation Authority) flats. I had a mattress with bed linen for travellers that I offered them if they were looking for a place to sleep, for free, in Mumbai. I hosted many Europeans and Americans in those days, and to their standards it was nothing, but I used to tell them before their arrival that I had an ordinary flat and only if they felt comfortable, should they then visit. During those arduous financial times, I was still open to share and help those travellers with the little I had. I always had to spend time and money when they were around, but that never stopped me from hosting them. Thus the excuse of 'unless you are rich, you cannot afford to share' is not true. There is always a possibility for sharing with others no matter how few resources you have, and having too much or too little is always subjective.

Once two Americans from New York visited my flat, and in this slum I lived in they were surprised to see people everywhere offering them free tea and food. They shared this experience with me, and for them it was unbelievable that people living in poverty could be so welcoming and sharing. The answer is however a simple one – they were generous.

Then there was another phase in my life when I

was working as an expat in Tanzania and doing well financially – and at that time I also hosted many people, in what was now a luxurious apartment with a private jacuzzi and a big swimming pool.

I would like to share a real incident that illustrates how an Afghan immigrant to Europe showed his benevolent nature. Shortly after I arrived on a trip to Copenhagen I visited a bicycle shop to ask for directions. After showing me the way, the owner asked me where I came from. When I explained that I was an Indian living in the UK, he immediately replied in Hindi. He started speaking fluent Hindi and told me that he had learned the language through watching Bollywood movies. Ever since the US invasion of Afghanistan he had been living in Copenhagen, where he was now running this bicycle shop.

Later our conversation switched to sociopolitical issues and he mentioned how fond he was of India and praised many things about the Indian government. He said, 'Apka PM Modi Afghanistan aaya tha, bahut madad ki hamari', which translates as, 'Your Prime Minister Modi came to Afghanistan and helped us a lot.' He told me how the Indian government had helped Afghanistan with the construction of the Salma Dam, which is expected to help Afghanistan once the Chabahar (India–Iran) project is completed, linking this Iranian port to Central Asia's road and railway networks.

At the end of our conversation when I asked him about the daily rent of a bicycle, he replied, '100 Danish kroner per day, but for you it's free'. I told him that I did not want the bike for free but he refused to take any money. He said that I could take his bike and return it on my last day. I wanted to give him either my ID card or passport number for surety, but he would not take anything. He only said, 'Aap pe vishwaas hai, jab man aaye tab wapas kar dena', which translates as, 'I trust you, and whenever you want to return the bike, please only do it then.'

In this way he gave me a free bicycle for five days, and his generosity and trust helped me to enjoy Copenhagen like a local. I am a Hindu by birth and he is a Muslim, but the link of peace and common humanity brought us together. On the strength of our first meeting he had shared something I was not expecting, and he did this without seeking anything in return. This shows that when human beings are bonded by love and peace, there is every possibility to share with strangers no matter what limited resources we have.

And in return, life offers you gratitude and happiness. While I was carrying out my trip around Europe I found friends everywhere, and on many occasions they provided me with free shelter and guidance. My trip became easier and I never felt distant from home. I never felt for a day that I was away from my country. And I think this was an outcome of the karma from my actions in India.

But to achieve the purpose of truly sharing we should practise the law of detachment. We should try to detach ourselves from the things that we love the most, and here I mean detachment from materialistic possessions. Start detaching from small things and then move towards big things. In the beginning it is difficult, but slowly, with practice, you will learn the art of detachment from wealth and you will also open up to sharing with others.

SHANTIH SUTRA 9

Practise Detachment

First stage
Breathe in and out 30 times with closed eyes, and then wait for one minute.

Breathe in and out 30 times with closed eyes, and then wait for two minutes.

Breathe in and out 30 times with closed eyes, and then wait for three minutes and proceed to the next stage.

Second stage: 10 minutes
Sit silently with closed eyes for 10 minutes, and then proceed to the next stage.

Third stage

Gift the material object that is closest to you. Find one material thing that you possess, to which you are too much attached, and give it to someone as a gift. This person could be a total stranger or someone in your outer circle of friends. You have to experience that your life will not end if you give away this possession, and in fact your life will still be very much the same. The object that you give away should be possessed only by you and it should not be shared with other people. For example, if you are living inside a house and it is the only house that you have and is where your family lives, then obviously you can't gift it, because otherwise where will everyone live? So the decision should be wise and not foolish. You can donate a big sum of money that was earned only by you, or a new car, or perhaps it is an irreplaceable favourite pair of shoes, suit of clothes, books, musical instrument, item of furniture, bicycle etc. Remember that you should never buy a new thing just to gift it. The sole purpose here is to move away from something you are attached to, and the attachment only happens when you are using something and are used to it – with time you will start believing that life is not possible without this object; therefore you have to break out of this thought process.

Detachment can be practised at a material or emotional level. But here, this exercise is focused on practising detachment at a material level, where you have to detach yourself from materialistic possessions.

· · · [10] · · ·

LOVE FOR THE ENVIRONMENT AND THE EARTH

My mother is Earth and I am her son.

Atharva Veda

There were a group of people who lived in a community and they considered themselves the best in all spheres of invention. With their advanced technology, they believed no one in this universe would be capable of destroying them. They were a rational and intelligent people and much obsessed with science, technology and innovation. They were in fact convinced that their skills had transcended nature, because they had built such powerful devices, spaceships and even robots capable of emulating human beings. They were convinced that they would always find a solution for any problem no matter how hard it was, and nothing could challenge their might.

But over the centuries their incessant interference with nature led them to the point from where it was difficult to go back and restore a harmonious system. The advancement in technology was marvellous indeed, but because it had been at the expense of nature it had destroyed the entire ecological system and slowly but inexorably the inhabitants of that island started to become extinct. A few concerned people who tried to make the others aware of this destruction at an early stage were quickly silenced by powerful and wealthy inhabitants, but silencing them was no solution because in the end the island was no longer habitable for living beings.

If we look around us in this world, we will observe that human beings are incessantly busy exploiting nature. We have taken our climate, water, air, plants, animals and birds, for granted. We exploit these for our own use. We have destroyed many forests, mountains, oceans and rivers, or polluted them with chemical toxins to the point where right now climate change is considered to be one of the biggest threats to human existence.

Already there are changes in temperature patterns throughout the world. Some countries are severely hit by drought and/or floods every year. In a few countries extreme weather conditions are causing thousands of deaths. The changes in weather patterns, and especially monsoon seasons, are adversely affecting farmers, agriculture, and peoples' livelihoods. This ongoing change in the environment will have a long-lasting impact on present and future generations.

Our obsession with nuclear power and the development of nuclear weapons has also destroyed our environment on a large scale. But many nations are still in the race to acquire nuclear arms without realising where it could lead.

Our disastrous acts have made many species completely extinct and even more are on the verge of disappearing. Out of greed, we kill elephants, tigers, lions, rhinos, whales, and many other species. We forget that if we respect our own life and freedom that they also have their own place in the world and we must respect their freedom too. They are like us, one unique species among millions in this universe. So if they don't interfere with us, then why should we harm them?

If human beings are more powerful and developed than other species, it does not mean they should take their liberty to exploit the rest.

In Africa I observed how certain Western tourists visit some African nations to eat the meat of endangered species. Once, when I was waiting for my flight at Nairobi airport, I overheard a conversation between two couples about how they missed eating giraffe meat. They were feeling sad that, after accomplishing most of the activities on their to-do list, they had missed out on eating the meat of the giraffe. There are a great many tourists who visit African or Asian countries, as their colonial forbears used to do, to hunt and eat the meat of exotic wild animals. It is unfortunate to see such human traits.

Unfortunately human beings consider everything in nature is there for their own purpose. So, to construct gigantic concrete buildings we destroy forests and then we neglect to plant trees elsewhere. The pollution of our industries has made many lakes and rivers poisonous and this has led to contamination of underground water reserves. Many rivers are no longer habitable by aquatic creatures. In the same way, hazardous gases have polluted the air and have given birth to many new diseases.

Our blind interference with nature has pushed us to the limit, so that in many countries a large proportion of citizens do not have access to free and clean drinking water. In many countries in Africa, and in developing countries around the world, there are millions who struggle every day to get clean water for drinking. Ideally clean drinking water should be easily available to every human being, but we have contaminated the water so much that in many countries, there is not enough clean water left for public consumption. And there are millions who cannot afford to buy water every day.

I would like to illustrate my point with the example of New Delhi, where my family moved in 1994, when my father received an army posting. Since that time, I have seen a major climatic change across this city. In the mid 1990s I remember that we used to have proper monsoons. On some occasions there was continuous rain for 3–4 days and our school used to give us a few days off. But by 2005–2006, the monsoon season had undergone a change. Nowadays during the monsoon season we only see rain once or twice a week, and for a very short period. This has made the local water level go down drastically and overall there is a shortage of water.

The quality of drinking water has also deteriorated and we have stopped drinking water directly from the tap. Either we buy clean drinking water, or use a water purifier before drinking. This was not the case when we had first moved to Delhi in 1994. In a similar way, the vast city of Mumbai has poor quality running water and most citizens have to buy clean drinking water every day. If we cannot have clean drinking water and fresh air to breathe, then it is going to adversely affect our physical and psychological health – our entire lives will become miserable.

We should try to connect the dots between saving our planet and lifting people out of poverty, climate change, water scarcity, energy shortages, and poor global health and food security – these are interrelated.

Unless we develop love for our environment we will not have a balanced life in harmony with it. So in the same way that we care for our own health and life, we must equally care for our environment. Sometimes we do not realise how much we receive from plants and trees at every moment and take their gifts for granted. For example we all breathe, but we never fully understand the essential daily process of breathing in and out, unless we stop for a few seconds and start to suffocate. So in the same manner if trees were to stop giving us oxygen, how could we exist? Without forests, water, mountains, rain, and clean air, there can be no life. And if we are not rooted in harmony with nature, then our madness for wealth, technology and concrete jungles will not lead us anywhere.

Over the past few decades we have started to explore new planets and in the coming decades it is even possible that we may start living on them, but it will be of no use if we start destroying their eco-systems in the same way that we are doing on earth. The most important necessity is for us to have peace, love, and a caring nature inside, and unless that happens we will not find peace anywhere, no matter where we get to or how well developed we become through technology alone.

Love and care for our environment is not a question of choice or ethics, but a matter of necessity and survival. We must care for our Mother Earth and we should love her in the same way we love ourselves. We should never forget that we exist through nature and not vice versa. We cannot exist without nature, but it can exist without us. We belong to the earth and earth does not belong to us. Unless we can develop this type of thought process and caring nature, we will not be able to stop our own destruction.

Together, let's promise that we will develop love for our planet, its environment, and all living beings on it. We must accept the fact that unless we develop such holistic practices, we will not be able to achieve overall peace and awareness. Our Mother Earth needs compassionate and kind-hearted human beings, and in return we will be blessed with peace and harmony.

SHANTIH SUTRA 10

Music

First stage
Breathe in and out 50 times with closed eyes, and then proceed to the next stage.

Second stage: 15 minutes
Sit silently in a relaxed position with closed eyes for 15 minutes, and then proceed to the next stage.

Third stage: 20 minutes
Find a silent place where you are sitting alone, as nobody else should be there to disturb you while you are practising this. Either listen to a classical instru-

ment, or play it for 15 minutes. Forget about anything around you, forget yourself and immerse yourself so much in the music that your physical body becomes insignificant. When it stops, keep sitting silently for at least five minutes more, and then this exercise is over.

Music, or sound, has an amazing effect on the human mind and spirit. Music is a very powerful tool to transform you from the inside out. Music can enrich your soul and help you to experience the eternal peace flowing inside and outside of you. Music is nothing but a sound, and sound is nothing except an expression of the universe communicating with you. Therefore, enjoy each vibration of sound while listening to or playing an instrument in this exercise.

HUMAN CONDITIONING AND RACISM

*A man, though wise, should never be
ashamed of learning more, and must unbend
his mind.*

Sophocles

At one time there was a small village on the shore of an island, and everyone in it was scared to visit the other side of the channel that separated it from the mainland. There was a story that whoever had gone to the other side never returned, and had disappeared forever. Every mother and father told this story to their children, and their children told the same story on to their children. Within a short time, generations of people were living with a fear of ever crossing to the mainland.

Soon people had been so conditioned by this taboo that they had stopped even thinking about the land on the other side. The entire village was living in its own world. Everyone was happily settled there with a simple living from the land and sea roundabout, living with their family and content to roam only within the vicinity of their island. Each villager was convinced that this one small island was the best place in the entire world.

But one day, a young man challenged the entire social system and amazed everyone by swimming across the channel. After a few years he returned alive and well, saying how he had explored a beautiful land vast in size, with many different landscapes and a more developed society. He narrated this story and inspired people of his own generation to cross to the other side, and in this way the isolated island life was transformed.

Human beings are deeply conditioned by their religion, nation, society and culture.

For example, in middle-class society, from the day we start going to school we are told, 'do something important with your life', and this means getting a higher degree, a good job, and making money. Our mind is conditioned with the thought of money from childhood: our parents tell us first about its importance, and then we see it everywhere we go. From our friends to our schools, to TV and billboard adverts, everywhere we are taught to earn plenty of money. And soon we fall into this trap. It happened to me, and it is happening to everyone every day, so you require a lot of courage to move out of this mindset and to think differently – it is not an easy path to choose.

I followed the same trend, at first when I focused on higher education and then again when I was hired by a big IT corporation. I worked with the world's biggest names in the IT–telecom industry and I held a good position for my age. But with time I got bored and wanted to move out; it seemed like I was only going to the office to receive my salary at the end of every month. If my salary was delayed for only a few hours or a day – I was getting restless. But I had been aware of my behaviour for many years, and I think it happens to everyone in the corporate world or in any routine job. The only difference is that I had started realising that I had to stop at some point – and that there was something beyond this.

This thought was boiling up in my head and, after I had plucked up enough courage, one day I decided to resign. That was a really big decision, as I was working from Mumbai with a big French IT consulting firm on a New York-based project. On the day I resigned, the director of the North American unit, who was based in Mumbai, called me and we had a face-to-face discussion. He tried his best to convince me to not resign. He offered me promotion, a salary hike, and even suggested that I go to work on the New York project at the client site in the US and stay there for three years – but I had already made up my mind. I wanted to discover myself and to move away from my monotonous routine job. He advised me to not make a hasty decision, but I turned down his offers and quit the job.

Wherever possible, live a life where your soul is not conditioned by society and money. We all need money to an extent and we definitely need it to pay the bills, but always be courageous enough to go off track, and if possible to take a sabbatical whenever you can. Sometimes it is better to volunteer with a non-profit organisation, a school, or work for free and you will realise – it adds so much meaning to your life – that you evolve as a better human being: you find the depth to your personality. Then your mind will not be conditioned by money, and you will not be scared by the thought of losing your job and career.

It often occurs that some people commit suicide during a recession. The reason is that they are so conditioned to their pay coming in regularly every month, they cannot imagine their life beyond this. They have taken everything so much for granted, their salary, their job, their savings, and when suddenly they lose it all, they go into a deep personal crisis. They are living under the burden of big loans or mortgages, and have become conditioned to luxuries that they cannot imagine doing without.

The only way to de-condition ourselves is to have the courage to step into new territory, and challenge our old conditioning.

In order to de-condition ourselves, we should not be shy about learning and making mistakes. A toddler falls many times when it starts walking for the first time, but eventually it gains enough strength and one day it starts walking and running on its own. In the same way we are like children in this universe – we will make many mistakes while learning a new language, dance, art, etc. but it does not mean that we should stop trying.

For example, learning a new language is a unique way to de-condition yourself and your mind. As we grow up in our society, we tend to think with its language and we become used to it. Our mind becomes comfortable with thinking only through that language, but once we start learning a new language we challenge our minds and begin breaking boundaries, and eventually we learn it. But unless we challenge our mind, we will never be able to do so.

In the same manner religious de-conditioning is important. If we are born into a Hindu family we should try to visit churches, mosques and gurudwaras, and if we are born into a Muslim family we should try to visit temples, churches and monasteries. Christians should do the same – and this way we can challenge our religious conditioning and open ourselves up to learn about a new belief system.

Sometimes it is also important to make people aware or to help them in their de-conditioning by presenting the other side of the story.

I would like to share an experience I had when I met an old couple in Edinburgh, Scotland while having my lunch at The Scottish National Gallery of Modern Art. After finishing my tour I was sitting alone inside the cafeteria, and was enjoying a delicious vegetarian soup and a sandwich. Later, an old couple came up to me and asked, 'If you do not mind, can we grab these chairs and sit here?' The cafeteria was packed and there were no other empty seats. 'Please help yourselves', I replied.

The man looked at my food and told his partner, 'This looks delicious,' and then asked me, 'what exactly are you eating?' I explained, and showed him the item on the menu. 'Great, then we will order the same.' Soon the conversation moved on, and they wanted to know where I was from. I told them I was from India, New Delhi, but right at that moment I was living and working in Bristol.

The man introduced his partner to me. The lady said, 'I have seen India only on TV. I have never been there, so my knowledge is limited to TV and movies, but I personally find your country fascinating.' She paused for few seconds and asked, 'If you don't mind, can I ask something from you? I've seen documentaries, and films too about India, like Slumdog Millionaire and The Best Exotic Marigold Hotel – so is India still poor?'

'Not really', I replied. 'Some people are poor, but not all over the country. It is a big country with a huge population and great diversity. So, we have some very rich people and also very poor people, with a big middle class in-between. It depends on what the media shows you. But the good thing is that India is doing pretty well and the middle class is growing every year.'

She considered this. 'I thought so', she said. 'Most of the time the media thrives on negative news or maybe this is just what people want to see.' She spoke politely with a gentle voice. 'But I like India for its meditation centres and peaceful messages. Buddha was from there? Is the 14th Dalai Lama also from India, or maybe he only lives there?'

I clarified that the Buddha was from India or Indian subcontinent, and that yes, the present Dalai Lama lives in India but originally he came from Tibet.

'Ok', she continued. 'Do you believe in re-incarnation and salvation?' I replied in the affirmative, and with a simple example I tried to explain to her what re-incarnation and salvation means in Hinduism and Buddhism.

Now her husband interrupted us. 'I would like to visit India, but at my age it's difficult to travel. Yet I would like to see the India of the British Raj. My uncle served under the Raj, and he used to tell us stories about India.'

'Really? What did he tell?' I asked him with curiosity.

He replied, 'Well, my uncle was in business, and once, after independence, he met the first Prime Minister of India. What was his name? Sorry, I do not remember.' He was struggling to remember the name.

'Mr Pandit Nehru', I said, helping him.

'Yes, that's the one. My uncle told me that he met Mr Nehru once when he wanted to do business in India. And it was easy to meet Mr Nehru as a British businessman in those days.

'We gave so much to India. What do Indians think about this?' he asked me.

'I don't think Indians like what you have given them', I replied to him with a smile.

Then his wife interjected, 'Don't worry, he thinks like a British person. It's not his fault.'

The man asked me again, 'But don't you think Great Britain gave many things to India?' As he was not going to desist, I tried to answer him diplomatically.

'Well, before colonisation the Indian subcontinent was one of the richest in the world. We were selling cotton, silk, spices and gold. Our contribution to world trade was enormous. The Indian subcontinent was generating more than 20% of the world's GDP (gross domestic product) before the East India Company took control of this region. But by 1947, the Indian subcontinent became one of the poorest on this earth, starving, helpless, struck with many famines and endemics. At the time of independence, India had an extremely low literacy rate, with no domestic industry and was deeply divided. So now you see the er ... British contribution.'

At this point, to reduce the tension, I started laughing. Actually, we all must have been feeling similarly as we all laughed together. But then I added more seriously, 'I am not saying these things without facts to back them up, for I was in Manchester museum a few months ago and there I discovered that after conquering India the British cotton industry flourished and the contribution of this industry to the UK's total export rose to almost 49% between 1834 and 1836, and then they started trading cotton across the entire world. They exploited cotton from the USA as well. The silk industry and spice industry reached its peak at this time and with it the UK became rich and had enough money to boost its industrial revolution. In fact this was partly how Britain became the world's wealthiest empire. I will not say it was only the Indian subcontinent that contributed to the British Empire because there were many other colonies, which the British Empire was exploiting. But, India was the brightest among all the British colonies.'

By now I held their attention with confidence so I didn't stop there, and continued, 'The famous British leader Winston Churchill called Mahatma Gandhi "The Naked Fakir." And in 1943 when the Bengal famine happened, and many Indian leaders and even British Administration employees approached him to help, his only reply was, "How come that Naked Fakir is still alive?" And in that famine, around 3–4 million Indians died.'

The man was now looking at me with a serious face and he nodded his head in acceptance. 'Yes, it's true. I read somewhere that he called Gandhi a "Naked Fakir", and it does not reflect well upon him.

'But we were in business. Some family members of mine got postings there in imperial government services. I think we put a stringent tax system on the Indian population that was not fair', he told me as I sipped my coffee.

'I completely agree with you Sir', I said. 'From your side you were not doing any wrong and the British East India Company was just doing business, of this there is no doubt. But part of the problem was at our end, because there was no unity in the Indian subcontinent. There were many rulers and they were selfish. India then was not like today's India and its unity was completely missing – there was no Indian national pride. And yes the businessmen from Britain used this opportunity, or as I should say, misused it – but anyway, it is a dirty past and personally I have nothing against anyone – the entire history of humanity is full of invasions and imperialism. Personally, among all the colonisers at that time I still think that the British rulers were the most organised, and at least when they left India you can claim that they left us with a democratic political structure. Many Indians will not agree with this view – but I think that this could be considered as a positive contribution. Also, they helped us to fight against Sati Pratha (the ancient practice where a widow would immolate herself on her husband's funeral pyre). Queen Victoria placed a complete ban on this. And not to mention, of course, the many atrocities committed by upper caste people to lower caste people and these were Indians doing this. And we should not forget that even England was ruled by Romans. It all depends on how far we want to go in human history. But one thing you can't ignore is that if the British Raj had not ruled the Indian subcontinent, this region would have been rich like many European countries.'

At this point the man looked at his wife and said, 'This guy is talking meaningful things and giving a different perspective.' Then he turned back to me and asked me what I did. I explained to him about my job in the IT–telecom industry. 'Impressive, we admire Indians for their intelligence and the way they are doing so well in IT', he said with a assertive tone.

'If you don't mind, can I ask you one question?' I asked him. 'Did you study the British colonial empire in India at your school?'

He thought about this. 'To be honest, not much', he said. 'Certainly nothing specific about India. We got it from our side; it was simply our empire all over the world and we only read about the good things. India was just one colony among many and we took pride in this.'

'I can understand,' I continued, 'that from your end things look different. You know, once I was invited to a flat in Amsterdam for a party. There I met a Dutch guy and he told me something interesting. We were standing on the terrace and he said as he waved his hand around the city – "Chit, all the wealth you see around you is made through atrocities on Indonesians, South Africans, Surinamese, and many other former colonial subjects. Sometimes I feel ashamed of our past, but sometimes I think that the luxuries I have today exist only because of this dirty past – and it gives me the freedom to study whichever subject I want to, for my government can help me with the funds. Hence, sometimes I am selfish and don't look at the past because I see it as not being my fault." And of course that guy was absolutely right', I told the couple.

'It is not the fault of today's generation for the injustices that happened in the past. If I was born in England, the Netherlands, or Spain, I would benefit from this ill-gotten luxury. So if you are born in a country, you will start looking at world affairs and history only from that angle and you will not try to see the other side, but as human beings we should try to. Personally, my attitude is based only on respect for human values, and only compassion, justice, non-violence, and love is going to solve the world's problems.'

'We agree with you', the woman replied, and both of them smiled.

'If in future,' I told both of them, 'you would like to visit India, please do let me know. I will try my best to help or at least guide you.' And the man said in reply that whenever I would like to visit Glasgow, I was to feel free to contact him.

He gave me his business card, and as he did so his wife said, 'It's not for business, it's because we liked talking to you so much and we would love to keep in touch.'

By looking at the man's card, I found out that he was a lawyer. When the bill came, he insisted that he pay my bill as well. I felt great while I was talking to this couple and appreciated the way that they showed a keen interest in knowing the other side of the story, and accepted the mistakes of the past. They were truly gentle, kind, and polite.

All human beings are driven by emotions, and conditioned by the society they were born and brought up in. Yet we should always make the effort to listen and to understand the other side of the story. If we do so, then we will help ourselves and the world. Because we are human beings, it is human values that must always be valued higher than any one religion, race or nation.

Since 2005, I have been working with people from all around the world. I have met people from different races, colours, religions and ethnic backgrounds, and I found that their behaviour is influenced by their social conditioning and upbringing.

It happened that some time ago, people were rude to me and tried to bring me down just because I am dark in skin colour. I wanted to react in that moment but instead I always held true to myself, because I believe that if you react with negative energy, it is not only going to harm you, but also the world. So it is better not to become angry, nor to show your negative energy in that moment, and if you are able to control it, after a few hours your anger will disappear.

There is a famous story about the famous Russian philosopher Gurdjieff. He said that throughout his entire life he followed the advice of his father, and this was to never express anger in the moment, but to wait for 24 hours. He practised this throughout his life and it worked for him, so therefore surely it could work for anyone.

If someone is racist towards you, it is best to ignore them because they are ignorant, and consider that they are not aware. By doing this you are not only helping yourself, but also the entire world. This way you can spread kindness and positive energy, peace and harmony, and in addition you will always be a happy soul. But here I am talking about individual incidents of racism and not about, say, a system where the laws promote it – if that is the case, then you will have to raise your voice in a peaceful manner, the way Abraham Lincoln, Mahatma Gandhi, and Martin Luther King Jr. did.

I will now take an incident from my own life. I was travelling in Kenya and was staying at Fisherman's Camp by Lake Naivasha, which is close to Nairobi. I was there with an Argentine friend whom I met during my stay in that city. We both decided to go for a bicycle safari in the day, and to camp during the night by Lake Naivasha. During my stay at Fisherman's Camp, I observed that everyone was white and that I was the only brown-skinned guy. In the night we all gathered for drinks and dinner and we were having many good discussions. Later on, another group joined us and it turned out they were from England and Australia. Our group was now made up of Britons, Australians, Kenyan-born whites, an Argentine, and myself from India.

Everyone was asked to introduce themselves and to shake hands. When my turn came, I introduced myself and a British guy shook hands with me, but afterwards when he went to shake hands with another British guy sitting next to me the latter said, 'Why are your hands stinking now?' At this, the first person replied immediately in a sarcastic tone, 'I just shook hands with Chit', and both laughed in a derisive way while looking at me.

In the moment I felt bad, but later on I forgave them and just dismissed them as being ignorant. Such meanness exposed their characters, but I decided to forget their behaviour and enjoy the evening instead of carrying any grudge.

Wherever it is possible in life, do not react. A reaction is a negative energy while acting is a positive energy. Anger against anger is a reaction, but if you behave calmly then that is a real action.

We need to accept that this world is not fair, and that you cannot expect everyone to treat you fairly. We cannot change the world or the way others think, but we can definitely change our own outlook and actions, and in this way we can make peace with ourselves and our surroundings. Because if every person was to start practising this, then in a few decades the world could become more peaceful and we would have more justice.

No matter how different our skin colour and culture is, the fact is that we all belong to the same earth, from the same species and have to live here together; there is no other option. So when we have to live together, then why not live peacefully? The day that we start treating others equally as 'human' – and sweep aside the barriers of religion, race, class, gender, sexuality, caste or culture – we will be able to find home, harmony and justice everywhere.

In life it all depends on how you see the world. It all depends on how you perceive and draw conclusions, and carry out your actions.

Do not forget that in the process of our de-conditioning (learning and unlearning), we not only help ourselves but also our entire society. Hence, do not get conditioned by the social world. Make an effort to detach yourself from the conditionings of your religion, race, nation, money or relationship: in this way you can experience true freedom and eternal peace.

SHANTIH SUTRA 11

Painting

First stage
Breathe in and out 50 times with closed eyes, and then
proceed to the next stage.

Second stage: 15 minutes
Sit silently in a relaxed position with closed eyes, and
then proceed to the next stage.

Third stage
Find a blank piece of paper and try to paint it with
all the colours or pictures that occur in your mind at
that exact moment. Painting is a powerful medium in

which to express your hidden feelings (sadness, happiness etc.), and in this way you will feel lighter and become more relaxed. You should not paint to show off your artistic skills, but only to experience yourself and the inner world that you have inside. Colours can express the universe to mankind. By painting, you can pour out your heart and mind. By painting colours, you ignite your mind and soul. While painting, enjoy using colours in the same way that nature fills the canvas of the earth with its mountains, rivers, trees and flowers of different colours and sizes. The entire exercise must be a peaceful and colourful journey, just like life. Keep drawing and painting whatever comes to your head, without thinking what you are painting or why. In the same way that thoughts come to your head without any logical reason, keep drawing and painting without any rational thought and enjoy yourself.

· · · [12] · · ·

EGO AND POWER

What good will it to do a man if he gets the
whole world for himself but loses his soul?

Jesus Christ

There was an emperor of the Indian subcontinent and he had inherited the vast Mauryan empire. But one rebel state known as Kalinga (present day Odissa in India) dared to withstand him and he marched against Kalinga with a big army and won the war. But this terrible conflict led to many thousands of deaths and is considered as one of the bloodiest wars in human history. At the end of the last battle when he inspected the battlefield, he found dead warriors and their widows weeping and cursing him – the entire battle field was covered in blood. This entire experience propelled him into deep remorse. Later he renounced his ego and hunger for power and became a Buddhist monk and spread Buddhism to many countries across the world. In this way he spent the rest of his life in the service of humanity. This man was none other than the famous king and warrior, Ahoka The Great.

Human ego works at a very subtle level and it is the root cause of most of the wars, misunderstandings, and differences that we see in world. No matter if the excuse used is your religion or a country or community, your ego fills you with this feeling that 'I am the best' and that your way is the best way to live life. Ego is nothing but self-pride, and it is also highly destructive. We are all living inside our own world of course, and it is true that not everyone will see this world and its problems in the same way, but if your mind is full of your own ego then you will become completely blind, stop listening to others, and become self-indulgent.

An uncontrolled ego creates an illusion that makes you think you are the best. If you are in a friendly

competition, like a game, and you want to outma-
noeuvre someone, then in this circumstance ego-
driven thoughts could work in a positive way. But
to approach life from the perspective of always being
in competition with others is a problem. Therefore,
those who want to conquer the world and wield power
strongly believe in and embrace their ego in what
they see as a positive manner, because it 'works' for
them. And it is logical to an extent, because if you do
not strongly believe in your ideas and think that they
are the best, you will struggle to convince others. But
ego also works as a catalyst to destroy others, to leave
everyone else behind, and to experience 'self-pride'.
That is the reason why we created so many conflict-
ing religions and political systems, because everyone
wants to prove that they have the best approach to life.

The ideologies of religions and nations are based
on the egos of their rulers or 'wise men'. Almost all
national anthems preach that their country is the best
and only their citizens are the blessed ones, because
if they did not inculcate such sentiments, then they
would not be able to inspire soldiers for their rulers'
wars. And if you read religious scriptures and listen
to the speeches of religious leaders, you quite often
discover that these too are only about boasting and
intolerance. They fill the adherent's heart with so
much dislike for others who have a different faith (or
none), that they stop appreciating others' thoughts,
and become convinced that this is the only path to be
followed. Your ego creates an amazing system with
well-defined rules and principles, and it leads you
towards a self-obsessed life. This creates enormous

hurdles for understanding other socio-religious systems.

Ego is the cause of many of the evils in this world. Ego is also the main cause of broken relationships and arguments. Ego promotes a conservative approach and does not allow you to think beyond the artificial boundaries it creates. It restricts you from exploring the best in life, which is often more easily available outside your limited world than within it.

There are many neighbouring nations that have fought each other for decades, and still there is no positive outcome. Some nations also got divided into smaller parts, but each in turn found itself facing the demand for ever smaller nations and regional autonomy. So there is no end to ego and its divisive nature. Once it begins, it keeps rolling on to its ultimate end and leads to dismay and misery.

Like the ideas of nations, each religion in the beginning came up with new philosophies that promoted peace, humanity and love, but soon they split into different sects within the same religion. There are Orthodox, Protestants, and Catholics within Christianity and each sect thinks it is better than the rest. In the same way, Islam has Sunnis, Shias, Ahmadis, and other small sects. These sects all have their distinct beliefs and practices, and unfortunately they can never find peace with each other. Hindus too have the caste system, and the upper caste exploit the lower caste.

The main idea behind racial, caste, and class systems is that a few people think they are better than others. People that identify together based upon, say, skin colour for example, unite on this basis and start believing that they are better than others. In the same manner the property owning or high earning groups in any nation or society create their own separate worlds and start discriminating against the low earning groups or those without property. The seed that leads to such folly is the ego. The class system, the caste system, and race-based systems are all just excuses and labels. The simple reason at the bottom of all this is the desire to feel better than others. Just to satiate the thirst of their egos, in the business world, competing corporate executives coin new names and tag lines for the almost-exact same product. So expensive brands, exclusive clubs and suchlike institutions exist and will keep arising again and again in the future, because the ego of a few will find an excuse to prove that they are better than the rest. It becomes the driving factor for one's existence. Soon you start working day and night just to earn more money, to attain more power so that you can feel better than other people. You always need someone to be compared with, and you will not enjoy the comparison unless you can show that you have more and are somehow different to the 'other'.

Again, we come up with our rankings of the richest countries, the most powerful men or women, the greatest nations, and form an exclusive group of the Great 7 or the Great 10 nations. And in this way we exercise our superiority over others. It becomes our driving force and to reach the pinnacle we do not care if we destroy millions of lives all over the world – ego lays the foundation of power and destruction.

Yet if we can master our ego, we will be free from

the desire of becoming the most powerful or richest person. Only then will we be enjoying each moment without thinking what others think and be more at peace. The more that we have ego-less people in the world, the better life we will have – instead of being obsessed with the rankings of the 'richest people' or 'the most powerful nations', we should promote and appreciate the wisest and most peaceful people on this earth, who are often its most marginalised and neglected – for if we do so, then we can have a more beautiful world to live in.

SHANTIH SUTRA 12

Dance with Madness

To perform this exercise you should first find a silent place where you are able to dance alone and can experience the joy that resides inside your soul. This exercise must be performed while you are standing upright. But please make sure that your music is not too loud, because you are playing this only for yourself and not for people who are living nearby!

First stage
Breathe in and out 50 times with closed eyes, and then proceed to the next stage.

Second stage: 10 minutes

Listen to some soothing music in a sitting position, as it should help you to go in deeper. Listen to this music for 10 minutes and start experiencing its effect upon your body and soul.

Third stage: 20 minutes

Now stand up and feel the sensation of this music, starting from your feet to your head. You must feel it in every part of your body. Slowly start moving your body, but only do this in a natural way. If you do not feel anything or have restricted mobility, then you can simply stand idle and concentrate on feeling. Do not start dancing for the sake of it. But once you do start dancing, then dance without thinking that there is someone watching you. Feel like you are the only person left on this earth. Feel like the whole of nature and existence is also dancing with you, and that it is happy to see you expressing so much joy. Forget about everything around you, and forget about yourself by immersing yourself so much that your physical body becomes insignificant.

Remember, you are not dancing to show your dancing talents to someone; you are only dancing to express the feeling inside you. There is no fixed pattern that you have to follow; you only have to move your entire body the way you feel in that moment. Just surrender yourself completely to the present moment and follow your soul. You mustn't wonder what others think when they see you dancing like this; you have to forget such thoughts completely.

For the whole period, dance with complete madness and reach the maximum limit that your body allows. Exhaust your body completely, and feel every single moment while you are dancing. Finally after 20 minutes of non-stop dancing, move to the next stage.

Fourth stage: 15 minutes

Now lie down on the floor, eyes closed, facing upwards with your hands open and your entire body in a relaxed position. Keep doing this for 15 minutes, and feel each breath coming in and going out. Experience your body not as you are inside your body, but observe it as if looking on from far away. If you practise this with total awareness you will experience that your body and soul are now separate. This enriching experience will make you aware and help you to understand yourself in better way. The more aware you become, the more active you will be in life. And the more active you are, the more you can contribute to the world.

POLITICAL SYSTEMS

*There comes a time when one must take
a position that is neither safe, nor politic,
nor popular, but he must take it because
conscience tells him it is right.*

Martin Luther King Jr

In a traditional society a woman once attempted to commit suicide, but survived. Later on, however, she was put on trial. The prosecution placed charges against her and the judge sentenced her to 20 years, because trying to commit suicide was seen as a severe crime. The judge said, 'Such people ... and most especially women,' he added, 'set a bad example for our society and are harmful to upcoming generations. Therefore this one should be severely punished as an example, so that no one will dare to attempt such an act in future.'

On the same day of the judgement, as it happened, the general election results were also announced and the country had a new president. Quickly this man established an authoritarian presidency and began instigating religious and ethnic violence inside the country to consolidate his power. Later on, he broke with the treaties that the former government had negotiated, invading countries to bring his beliefs and style of 'peace' to other regions.

This president ruled the country for 20 years. Finally, the majority of people realised that their president was a foolish and barbaric man who had filled their lives with violence and hatred, so once his wars had come home to wreck their own country, they overthrew him. But by this time, of course, enough damage had already been done.

Meanwhile the woman who was imprisoned for 20 years lived her entire life in solace, in a humble and peaceful way and she also wrote a book. When she got out of jail she tried to publish her work, but no publisher would touch it because she was, in their eyes, a crazy person and a former prisoner to boot. The most common reply was, 'Who the hell is going to read you? Be serious. A woman with suicidal tendencies can't be an inspiration for others – how ridiculous! Go and find yourself something better to do.'

So in time this woman writer died, but later on her book was published by an unknown publisher who had recognised the wisdom of her words.

Through publication the book slowly became very popular: it revolutionised people and made them aware. Her work was finally adopted as part of her country's school system, and she became a role model for many of the youth.

And one day, a follower created a revolutionary political movement in her name.

Most human beings are too short-sighted to see the future, or certainly, a better future. It also becomes difficult to explain what a better future might be. But to put it in simple words, a better future is one where there is justice, equality, and freedom, and where all citizens have a peaceful life and a transparent legal system that protects them.

Unfortunately, politics is dominated by egocentric people and those who are filled with hatred. It is difficult to find political heroes who are not promoting some form of hatred or intolerance. If they belong to a political party then they start talking negatively about other parties: that is how they express their opposition. If the party leader is seen as a national figure, then they start criticising neighbouring countries and this is how they seek to unite their countrymen.

Ironically , hate has always been the most important catalyst for unity. During war we fill our hearts with hate for others and that is the only way to wage war and win it. So we rant and rave, using vicious words against communities that we want to defeat. We galvanise our energy day and night to spread negative thoughts among our followers about how these others are wrong, and that we have to go and correct them.

The brutal fact of the political world is that if you are not egotistical, then you will never reach the top of any political party or community. Unless, day and night, you believe that you are the best and that your political party and/or nation is the best, it is hard to become a chief and find followers. And of course once you reach the top, then you start expanding your power into other areas, and it never stops. After one nation is in your power, you may wish to conquer other nations and then the entire world. You are always finding new phrases to denounce those who do not listen to you. You play with the words of democracy, communism, nation, etc. You come with all the best grand-sounding platitudes that can be exploited to justify maiming and torturing people.

If your opponent is small and weak, you can destroy him easily. But if your opponent is powerful and reluctant to follow you, you bring like-minded nations together, form a union, and then destroy that enemy either through war or by preventing its economic growth. This is nothing new; it has been happening for centuries, and only the forms are different.

But if you ask why we do this, the only reason I can find is that human beings are egotistical, violent, and greedy species. As their desires are never-ending, so are their sufferings and miseries.

There is no one perfect, single political system that is going to solve all these miseries. In the hands of politicians, democracy, communism, and socialism are just phrases to play around with and used to distract the citizenry. Every system has its flaws, and no single one can fix all the issues. Unless a system provides equal opportunities for all to grow in their lives, it is not going to serve its intended purpose – and this is the risk of all political systems. We cannot justify a political system just by repeating its phrases and slogans.

There are always contradictions in political systems – for example, many rich countries formed democracies, and yet they destroyed other countries in a dictatorial way. At the same time there have perhaps been a few enlightened dictators who provided peace and prosperity to their citizens, but of course most were mass killers who hungered after power. In the same way there have been communist regimes that while they brought health and some form of security to the poor, have simultaneously destroyed faiths and cultural traditions in a brutal manner and propagated a dictatorial agenda.

The truth is that, in the same way that olive trees cannot grow everywhere or vineyards perform well under all temperatures, and that one religion is not everybody's solution, one single political system cannot be applied across the world. Every society has its own cultural roots and conditioning, and is based upon its own historical experience. Therefore as a society evolves, its political system should also keep evolving, and it should be ready to learn from other societies. During each century in the future we will see new political forms arise, but the base of each should be only compassion, equality, justice, freedom and honesty. If this is lacking, then no system can serve its citizens.

For any political system, the ultimate aim should be to provide an 'honest, transparent, sustainable system'. We must remember that no single political group has the ultimate solution. Political needs are different because human beings are constantly changing, their lifestyle and thought processes are changing, and therefore some theory that was written a few centuries ago likely will not be applicable now. We need to keep refining our own political systems based upon changing societal needs and experiences.

The political system that fits a given culture will not necessarily fit another one. Every society and culture has its own thought processes and only a political system based on that will be sustainable. Leaders from far away nations should not try to enforce their political views on a different culture, for if they do so, they will destroy its checks and balances and its already existing political culture, while creating chaos in the lives of millions of its citizens.

I have been to democracies like the USA and former communist nations like Russia – and I saw good and bad in both. There is always something good to learn from almost any type of political system.

Even though comparison between different political systems is inevitable and should occur, such comparisons must be based on the intention of learning positive things from the societies being compared.

By practising this, we will see fewer clashes and more peace and harmony in this world. Societies will flourish together and keep learning from each other continuously, and in such a way we can make the earth more peaceful. When different political systems start to appreciate each other and open their windows, they will welcome in new possibilities and the mutual development of all.

SHANTIH SUTRA 13

No News

First stage
Breathe in and out 30 times with closed eyes, and then sit silently for one minute.
Breathe in and out 30 times with closed eyes, and then sit silently for two minutes.
Breathe in and out 30 times with closed eyes, and then sit silently for three minutes and then proceed to the next stage.

Second stage: 10 minutes
Sit silently with closed eyes for 10 minutes, and then proceed to the next stage.

Third stage: 3 days

Today, promise yourself that you will completely cut yourself off from reading, watching or listening to any type of news from any source for three days in a row. You have to de-condition yourself from too much worldly information. By not watching, listening to or reading news of course you will not be able to influence or even observe the world, but it will help to de-condition you from your society and find more peace inside yourself. Too much information often leads to too much stress and distraction. We do not require so much information, and we certainly do not need to know everything that is happening in the world. The important thing is what we are doing in our daily lives and how we are contributing positively to the world. Most news is full of negative or frivo- lous coverage and it is not healthy for your mind to keep hearing about such stuff. Therefore try to detach yourself completely from TV channels, newspapers, social media, radio, etc.

Also try not to indulge in any type of political or social gossip with your friends or family. If for three days you ignore such talk, you are very unlikely to miss anything important. The time will instead allow you to connect with yourself, and you will experience that a lack of information and any subsequent debate about it, whether this is internal or external, means more peace. Hence, practising such aloofness and silence while still living in our busy world, for at least three days, will bless you with peace. If possible, practise this for more than three days or for as long as your lifestyle, work, mind and soul allows you to.

· · · [14] · · ·

WAR AND PEACE

The two most powerful warriors are patience and time.

Leo Tolstoy

One day during FIFA 2014, Germany was playing and I decided to go and watch this match in a pub with friends. I found a German football shirt that I had bought in India before the start of FIFA matches. I was supporting the German football team and had decided to wear this on the day when the Germans were playing against the English team. I was looking for a pub but almost all looked packed, yet finally I found one pub that had some space left to sit and watch this game.

Since I was in Bristol it was obvious I would see more British people inside that pub than any other nationality. When people saw me in a German shirt many looked at me in a very scathing way, while a few smiled at me in a derogatory manner. I could empathise with them because being an Indian wearing a German football shirt, and sitting among British white folks, might be seen as being not respectful to them; but in a democracy you surely have the freedom to choose which football team you like to support.

When I ordered a drink the waiter said, 'Good to see at least one German supporter here', to which I asked him, 'Are you from Germany?' He took the order and looked around. 'No, I am Portuguese, but I am supporting the German team today.' He said this with a meek voice and left.

It might be possible that because of their history, the British are not fond of Germany and especially when it was a FIFA match. For every attack from the English side, people were shouting and cheering. Sometimes they looked at me as well, to express their belief that they were going to defeat the team I was supporting. But I was unfazed and enjoying the game. The German attack was better and they were playing with a good strategy – since the beginning they had been dominant overall and in comparison the English football team's tactics were feeble.

During half-time I observed that a fairly old man was looking at me. He came to me and asked, 'Would you mind if I ask where you come from?' and I replied that I was from India. Then he said, 'I don't believe in race, colour, nation or anything, but I don't like Germans. I hate them.'

He said this and returned to his seat. I didn't bother to ask him why he didn't like Germans because I knew this subject was controversial and it was better to enjoy the game than to enter into any such discussion. I was there to watch a game and not to discuss sociopolitical issues.

But later, when the German team scored a goal, he spat out bad words against the German team and stared at me. This was not helpful because I was becoming little bit uncomfortable as the only person there who was openly supporting the German team. When you are in a visible minority you are always vulnerable, especially when you know that you are in someone else's territory.

I thought it was better to ask him why he had so much hate against this country, so after building up enough courage I asked him, 'May I know why you don't like Germans?'

At this, he immediately jumped from his chair and came close to me. He was in shorts with a blue shirt and dark-coloured hat. He was tall, looked sporty for his age and was eager to give a reply. He started babbling, 'They think they are the best. They are an arrogant people. It's true they are good in making cars and other things, but my grandfather was in the British army and during the Second World War he was killed by German soldiers.'

'Sorry to hear that', I replied, but in the back of my mind I was thinking 'your grandfather was not in that war to *play poker.' Because I am quite sure that he was there to kill other people for similar reasons that he was himself killed.*

This old man was still carrying something in his heart that had allegedly happened many decades before and was living a life full of prejudice against the entire German nation because of it. He was hating people of one nationality for no reason and was spreading this negativity both inside himself and around him. The German and British kids who are born today have nothing to do with the past and they are not responsible for the wars that happened back then. We should not label a society because something happened in the past or because one person from one community did something wrong against you. The British government ruled India for more than 200 years but I have nothing against them. The past is often unpleasant, yes, but we have to move on in life.

Wars are like two opposing teams fighting for truth and justice. But truth and justice are subjective. It is not like science where 1+1=2 for everyone, no matter if you are French, German, Chinese, Hindu, Muslim, Christian, or Jewish.

Human beings often form groups and they believe that they are the best or at least better than the rest. And whenever we create a group we create stringent hierarchies and this leads to an ego tussle. Since you cannot convince everyone of what you believe in, you will attract retaliation from the other side, and while trying to convince them, most of the time you will fail – and when such failure reaches extreme levels, war breaks out.

If you bomb a nation that is far away and you think that you can live in peace, it is not going to happen. Sooner or later, the consequences of the destruction you wreaked will affect you as well. Or if you think that you can poison another land and steal its resources for your own benefit, it will not turn out this way. Those who are left suffering in these far-away places will sooner or later come knocking at your door – this situation has been experienced many times in this world.

War is such a complex subject that we can spend time discussing and trying to justify its existence, but in the end we can conclude that it is negative for any society at any given time. I believe that deep inside every human there is violence looking for an excuse to act out.

We have seen war between capitalism and communism, or perhaps in the name of democracy against a regime labelled as authoritarian, or fascist. Each opponent tries to defy the other and strongly believes that their way is better.

Whenever I ponder on this subject I find that, as there is a serious existential crisis inside every human being, this leads to a crisis in every society or nation. There is a strong sense of pride and ego within each human, and this makes them take extreme steps. This kind of behaviour makes them come together to create a new society with new rules, and from this they claim that they are the best. In time they try hard to establish themselves economically and politically, and once they grow big, they start trying to spread themselves across the world. There is a kind of self-gratification and happiness they experience in their hearts when they see their millions of followers. The founders of such philosophies, in time, become heroes and may get worshipped as a God or Prophet. Then these artificial Gods and their messengers start destroying other beliefs, and this always leads to war. This perilous attitude has been deep inside every human since time first began.

The question is, 'Is there a permanent solution that can move the world away from its wars? Is there going to be a time when we will not see any wars on this earth?' The honest answer is that there may never be a time when there are no wars. But it is possible for humanity to see fewer and fewer wars. For example, if today we see one new war a year, maybe we can reach the level where we will see only one war in 50 years, and that would be a great achievement.

People will always argue that some wars are necessary. When you see an evil regime that is committing atrocities against its own countrymen and is not willing to listen to its citizens or outside forces, then theoretically it might be necessary to intervene through war, but only in the rarest of scenarios might this be applicable. We need to take strong action against evil leaders, but again it is subjective about who is evil and who is the 'messenger of peace'. Who is going to decide this? The powerful will always find some excuse to justify their actions. Therefore it becomes highly subjective and depends on our interpretation of the context and the way in which we analyse the situation.

The only solution that I can see is to fill your own heart with justice, compassion and the principles of non-violence; this is the only way to bring peace to this earth. We should become wiser from inside first and this will only happen when we stop filling ourselves with self-pride and ego, and start treating others with justice without passing judgement – for if we do so, we can create an amicable society on earth and have fewer wars.

SHANTIH SUTRA 14

Gibberish

Find a peaceful place inside your house, or a garden, or anywhere where there is no distraction so that you can sit silently and practise speaking gibberish.

First stage
Breathe in and out 30 times with closed eyes and then sit silently for one minute.

Breathe in and out 30 times with closed eyes and then sit silently for two minutes.

Breathe in and out 30 times with closed eyes and then sit silently for three minutes and then proceed to the next stage.

Second stage: 11 minutes

Close your eyes and start saying something nonsensical (gibberish) continuously for five minutes. Gibberish is speaking something in a language that you do not know; words that have no sense, no grammar, no meaning at all. For example, if you are German, you do not say anything in German or in any other language you know. You can say something that you heard somewhere once but only if you just remember the sound but do not understand a single word of it.

For example, you might try to speak in Chinese, but remember that if you do you should not know the meaning of any word of Chinese. However, you could use the Chinese accent or linguistic sounds that you have heard somewhere.

The ground rule is that you do not have to try to do anything, but just start forming words and speaking nonsense continuously. Once you begin, do not stop, even if you are short of words, so keep saying something and slowly you will find your way. Keep saying whatever words that come into your mind. For help, observe toddlers and see how they say something that does not make any sense and see how they keep talking non-stop to communicate with others. They speak based only on the sound they observed, without following its grammar or meaning.

Please practise the above in two parts, each of five minutes, with one minute of silence in-between. This must be practised in a sitting position with your eyes closed.

Third stage: 5 minutes

Sit silently for five minutes with closed eyes.

Gibberish is a powerful technique invented by the Sufi mystic called Jabbar. Every human has a desire to say something and they enjoy it when more people listen to them. Everyone's mind is full of thousands of thoughts that simultaneously exist at any given time. So when we practise gibberish we are throwing all those words outside ourselves and also fulfilling our desire to keep talking non-stop, but the listener is the same person who is speaking. This does three things – you throw garbage out of your mind, you say something non-stop, and you keep listening to yourself. In this way your mind becomes empty for a period, and during this moment of emptiness you experience real silence. And when your mind is empty then only fresh thoughts appear, and you are able to enjoy the present moment. Gibberish empowers you and, in a simple and subtle way, it cleanses your mind.

You can practise this alone or in a group. If you are in a group and feel shy about practising together, each person can try sitting separately facing a wall in the meditation room and practise this way.

THE SPIRITUAL WORLD

SELF-REVOLUTION AND SOCIAL REVOLUTION

Knowing yourself is the beginning of all wisdom.

Aristotle

Two thousand years ago there was a prince in India and he had all the luxuries that you can imagine. He was happy with his life and he indulged himself in all forms of materialistic pleasures. But one day something revolutionary happened – while he was on a journey and passing along a road, he observed a few things for the first time in his life: a dead body, an old man, and a diseased man. In that moment he started to ask himself questions and the replies he received changed him forever. He left his kingdom and his wife and began wandering to seek the truth. After wandering for 11 years he finally achieved enlightenment, and in that moment he not only revolutionised himself but also the whole world. This man was none other than Mahatma Buddha, who was born under the name of Siddhartha.

A revolution happens at two levels: revolution of the self, and social revolution. Now the question is – which happens first? If you observe human history, most of the time people attempted to bring social revolutions to change the world first. These social revolutions were driven by religion, politics, or economics. A social revolution is easy to understand, and it is easy to get caught up in it: it creates a ripple in the mind and the sensation of euphoria. It gives hope that dreams are going to be fulfilled and that miseries will be over soon, forever. It creates a mass movement and sudden turbulence in society.

Throughout human history revolutions have occurred many times and they caused wars, changed governments, divided nations and gave birth to new nations or communities. Such wars happened across Asia, Africa, Europe, and The Americas. We fought those wars in the hope that they would bring social reforms and that things would be sorted out; but in the end there were many disappointments. Human beings are just as restless and full of misery as before; maybe you could, perhaps, argue that the situation is even worse. Still we see injustice after changes in government or in social relations. The leaders who brought revolution by selling the dream of justice became corrupt and soon forgot what they had promised, as did the common people. Ordinary people cannot keep protesting for their entire lives, so after a few days or months or years of struggle they lose heart and go back to their routine. They enter into a dormant mode, and then after a few decades a new uprising or revolution breaks out with new promises and once again the same thing happens. A few opportunists usually take advantage of the situation, seize a position of power and start doing the same thing as their predecessors. So unless social revolution is combined with revolution of the 'Self', people will keep looking for a new mirage to follow, and this will never end.

When I was working with the India Against Corruption movement, which was considered to be the biggest social movement after India gained its independence in 1947, I learned many things about how this movement worked. I was a full-time volunteer; we were trying to make India a corruption-free country, and this idea inspired millions of people across the land. When it was at its peak, hundreds of thousands of people all marched together. I still remember one beautiful evening when more than 150,000 people

marched towards one of the wealthiest neighbour-
hoods, Juhu in Mumbai. Mayank Gandhi was the
leader of Maharashtra (a state in Western India),
and I was working with him. He was the face of the
anti-corruption movement in Western India and it
was my job to handle social media and email press
releases to the media. This opportunity to work with
well-known social activists in India was a once-in-
a-lifetime opportunity, and it made me a different
person. Everyone was working selflessly and there
were people from different groups of society – street
vendors, working men and women, college students
and business people, etc. – everyone wanted to see an
honest, corruption-free India. As time passed however,
this movement became big and a professional core,
or elite, emerged, just like a political party. In the
beginning all the leaders were saying that they would
never form such a party, but this is what happened
eventually.

I would like to call up one specific example that
exudes how trivial issues come into play while trying
to bring about profound social reforms, and show how
such small issues can create rifts within the movement
or political party.

One evening Mayank Gandhi and I went to meet a
team of squabbling volunteers in Thane, a district in
Western Mumbai, to sort out their differences. Since
we were in the core team for Mumbai, we had to go
and listen to them. The complaint had come to me
first – the volunteers wanted to meet Mayank Gandhi.
I told Mayank about this and he decided to go and
talk to them, although he was extremely busy. When

we reached the location, the atmosphere was pretty tense. There were two groups already formed into antagonistic teams, and we could feel it the moment we arrived. The leaders of the two sides were not prepared to speak to each other. When we started listening to the larger group, their complaints were about how the people from the smaller group did not share the money being spent on buying samosas and tea, or arranging evening meetings etc. The complaint was that the smaller group had private meetings, and did not message the entire group about them. Some leaders, it was claimed, did not share their knowledge about where protests were going to happen and after-wards only sent photographs of their 'private' event to the central team. It was also stated that the real volunteers never got a chance to speak to the media and they felt dejected about this.

Because of the smaller team's opportunistic behaviour and the subsequent ego fighting, a damaging rift had already been created within the Thane team of volunteers. I saw a big contrast – at one end they were all trying to fight against the corrupt establishment and at the other end and within their own social movement, corruption was taking root once more.

After listening to the complaints, I realised that when such things started happening at such a basic level, perhaps the same would occur when India Against Corruption became a political party. The story would remain the same, and it would become just like any other political party. So the problem is not with the political party or social revolution per se – the problem is that while every human is primarily self-centred and brings about a revolution, forms a political party, or creates a religion without first looking inward, it ends up with the same result. This is exactly what happened to this particular movement and to its organisation in the end.

If you look back on the past, you will observe that after every few decades a new leader tries to bring about a social revolution and millions follow him. It happened in the past, and it will keep happening in the future. It is a human trait, for change is constant, and we try our best to bring about change in the outside world. But the irony is that, why, after so many revolutions and big promises, couldn't we stop the basic problem? Why do we still see so much poverty, hunger, injustice, sickness and violence in the world?

Why did these social leaders with their grand ambitions not achieve as much as they might?

Because, if you go deeper and analyse human society, you will find that only a few things are going to stay forever in this world – greed and violence for sure, but also peace and love. Most of these social movements (whether communist, socialist or democratic) aimed to bring prosperity and social change, but ended in either corruption and failure or limited success only through chaos and violence. So is there a way to bring about a long-lasting change without these negative side effects?

The answer is yes. It is possible, but only through a self-revolution or spiritual revolution. If you examine human nature you will see that self-revolution is the most powerful tool with which to spread peace and justice. Self-revolution is a spiritual revolution and it happens at an individual level, so it does not force something on others. Whenever you try to enforce something on others you need violence, power, and propaganda, and then it is difficult to see love and peace, as the only space left is for war and conflict. Self-revolution is a spiritual journey, while social revolution is a political journey. The former journey is also one that goes inside, whereas social revolution is a journey on the outside. In self-revolution you are alone, and you do not need others. In a social revolution you need a crowd and big gatherings and it is dependent on others. And whenever hundreds of thousands of people are involved in a social revolution, unless they are also on the same path, whatever truth it holds will soon be lost. You cannot find truth in a herd – for in this instance the individual, and also the truth, stands alone.

Mahatma Buddha is the best example. Before becoming Buddha (The Enlightened One) he had to undergo internal conflict and deep questions about his existence and that of the world and universe. On this journey he wandered alone for 11 years, until finally at the age of 40 he attained enlightenment. Later he started travelling with his students, giving lectures as he spread peace and love throughout the world. He did not kill a single person in this process. His words of wisdom attracted people, and more than 30 countries adopted his teachings. His self-revolution was so deep that he touched the lives of billions of people. He did not force his thoughts on others; he said things peacefully as if there was no one to listen, but his words were so rich and meaningful that his teachings were accepted everywhere. In this way he brought about the biggest social revolution. Because, if a social revolution is driven by a spiritual revolution where nobody is forced to accept dogmas or rules, then its impact will be everlasting.

In recent times, Mahatma Gandhi is the best example. His movement for freedom was a result of the deep spiritual wisdom he had attained. His social movement helped force the British government to leave India, and he achieved this without hurting anyone. He campaigned solely through his peaceful speeches and by following the principles of non-violent resistance. Martin Luther King Jr and Nelson Mandela later followed in the footsteps of Mahatma Gandhi.

We can practise this voyage of self-discovery in our day-to-day lives and can see the changes. Instead of changing things outside first, if we only change our nature, then the way we perceive and see things will alter accordingly, and the entire world will become beautiful. Therefore the key to change is in self-revolution, and this will lead to a social revolution that embodies eternal peace and harmony.

SHANTIH SUTRA 15

Vipassana

Vipassana (insight meditation) means to know yourself. Insight meditation is an observation of your true self. Like Buddha, unless we know and discover ourselves, by seeking outside, we cannot find happiness. Unless this realisation happens, we cannot achieve peace. Buddha himself taught this practice and it is considered as one of the most important practices among Buddhist traditions.

The radical insight comes from discovering that our happiness does not depend upon manipulating the external world.

Vipassana meditation is a discipline for purifying

the mind of the elements that cause pain and suffering. Vipassana meditation teaches us to 'be in the moment' and experience the body and mind with complete attention to both.

The word 'vipassana' has two parts – 'Vi' and 'Passana'. The prefix 'Vi' in the Pali language means the special way, and the meaning of 'Passana' is to see, to observe, or perceive. And if we combine both words together, it means to see and experience things intensely. It is an immediate insight experienced before one's eyes and has nothing to do with reasoning or thinking.

Through Vipassana we try to observe ourselves and the existence around us through deep concentration. We practise being in the moment and observing all the elements – earth, fire, water, air, smell, colour, and taste.

The exercise below is going to help you observe life around you and to relive each moment as an observer. This meditation is a full day exercise and must begin at six o'clock in the morning.

First stage
Breathe in and out 50 times with closed eyes, and then sit silently for two minutes.

Breathe in and out 50 times with closed eyes, and then sit silently for three minutes and then proceed to the next stage.

Second stage: Gibberish (10 minutes)
Close your eyes and start saying something nonsensical (gibberish) continuously for five minutes.

Gibberish is speaking something in a language that you do not know; words that have no sense, no grammar, no meaning at all. For example, if you are, say, German you do not say anything in German or in any other language you know. You can say something that you heard somewhere once but only if you just remember the sound but do not understand a single word of it.

For example, you might try to speak in Chinese, but remember that if you do you should not know the meaning of any word of Chinese. However, you could use the Chinese accent or linguistic sounds that you have heard somewhere. This powerful technique will help you to cleanse your mind.

Third stage: 30 minutes
Sit silently with closed eyes, observing your mind and the thoughts coming into it like an outsider – do not fight these thoughts – let them appear and just observe them as you observe the outside world with your eyes open.

Fourth stage: Eating breakfast (30 minutes)
Have a light breakfast and enjoy each bite – eat each portion with love and compassion. Chew very slowly and let your tongue, jaw, teeth, stomach, heart and mind enjoy each moment spent while eating. Eat as slowly as possible.

Fifth stage: Silence (120 minutes)
Just remain silent and do not speak, read, write or communicate to anyone through any means. Either

keep sitting idly or lie on the floor, and observe each breath coming in and going out. The entire focus must be on watching and enjoying your breathing process – but make sure that you do not fall asleep while practising this.

Sixth stage: Walking (30 minutes)
Go for a walk, but walk very slowly – your walk must be at least five times slower than your normal walk. While walking, observe every move, every step and every sensation starting from your feet, then moving to your waist, shoulders and head. Feel every muscle that is working when you walk, and keep saying thanks in your mind to each body part that helps you to walk. Choose a path to walk on and keep going round (depending on its length) for 30 minutes. But please make sure that you maintain complete silence throughout this walk, and it is better if you practise this alone and not at a busy place so that you do not get distracted or disturbed. It is best to practise this technique in natural surroundings, but you can do it inside your house as well. The thirty-minute walk must be enriching and should not be done with haste, as every move must be observed and enjoyed carefully.

Seventh stage: Eating lunch (30 minutes)
Have a light lunch and enjoy every bite. We can turn eating into another meditation, with the primary object being the sensation of taste. Since we often eat while doing other things, such as reading, watching

something or talking to other people, this time we have to eat with complete concentration.

Insightful meditation is not limited to formal periods of sitting and walking, but it can be extended into more and more of our activities during the day. Physically slowing down helps to keep us more grounded in our bodies, and lessens the distracting effects of fast-moving thoughts.

All of these practices aim to develop a calmness that unveils our capacity to experience things as they really are. This direct experience leads to genuine happiness, to freedom from suffering.

After lunch, walk again for 10 minutes so that you will not fall asleep during the next stage, or if possible have some green tea (no sugar or milk), so that your mind will be fully alert when you practise the silent, sitting meditation.

Eighth stage: Sitting (60 minutes)

Sit silently with closed eyes, observing your mind and the thoughts coming into it like an outsider – do not fight these thoughts – let them appear and just observe them like you might observe the outside world with your eyes open.

Ninth stage: Observing (60 minutes)

Observe nature or yourself by doing nothing. You could be lying on the floor or the bed, sitting in front of a window and looking outside, sitting in a forest looking at trees, at the birds, at some mountains, a river or flowers, or just sitting inside your room looking at a picture on the wall, observing every detail.

Tenth stage: Keep silent until the time you sleep
Maintain silence for the remaining hours of the day and do not speak, read, write or communicate to anyone through any means until the time you go to sleep. If possible, go to sleep early.

If you have successfully practised the above exercise, please try it again many times in the future. It could be practised at home, but preferably the ideal location would be to practise somewhere away from home and from the madness of busy cities, somewhere close to nature, or at a retreat. If that is not possible, then you will need to practise it at home with a focused and disciplined mind.

Once you are comfortable with practising this exercise for a single day, next practise it using the same techniques and enthusiasm for two days in continuation, then for three days, and keep on increasing the number until you can manage 10 days. Finally, if you wish, go on a meditation retreat and complete a 10 day Vipassana course under ideal conditions.

This exercise aims to help you to stretch your limits step-by-step, test your boundaries and calm down the noise and restlessness inside you – for, once Vipassana is successfully experienced, the entire world will look peaceful because you have found peace within yourself.

· · · [16] · · ·

EXPERIENCE

The purpose of life is to live it, to taste experience to the utmost, to reach out eagerly and without fear for newer and richer experience.

Eleanor Roosevelt

In Madrid, when the door of the metro train opened, a little girl of about 2–3 years old entered and started shouting in Spanish, 'Asiento, asiento, asiento (seat).' The metro was full of people and there was no seat to sit on. Then she started jumping and crying while her father and mother looked on helplessly. Finally a woman stood up and offered her seat to the little girl. At this, she suddenly became happy and jumped on the empty seat and started gazing out of the window.

In life, many times we crave little things and sometimes spend our entire lives chasing them without realising it, even though, in this vast universe, their existence is negligible. But our behaviour is similar to this little girl who felt pain, in that moment, for a seat – to adults her behaviour looked childish. In the same manner, when we grow higher in human consciousness we also encounter the same sort of experiences, but unless we pass through them, this realisation never happens.

In my early 20s I had a desire that the world should know me, but today I only want to know myself, and each day I am engaged in self-discovery. During my teenage years and early twenties I wanted to change the world, but today, I only want to change myself and the way I see the world. This has brought more peace into my life and it gives me happiness. The desire to be listened to, the desire to be known and to get recognised, has been kept in proper balance ever since the day I started to know myself.

The more you go outside, more distracted you will become, but the more you go inside, the more peaceful you will become; the choice is yours. It is up to you what you want to achieve in life. The desire to change the world and the thought that people around you should conform to your wishes and ideas is not going to happen. I have learned this with experience.

It is important to learn life's lessons through real experiences: in this way you develop your human consciousness more profoundly. You should not believe something simply because it was told to you by your parents and your society. You should explore on your own, and for that you need to travel an arduous path through the predicaments of life, and in this way you become more aware.

When I was travelling in Moscow one evening, I decided to take a train and go out of the city and cut away from the tourist traps, to see how people far away from the city centre lived. I boarded the train and when I reached the last station I started walking around outside. It was a cold March night and the roads were covered with snow. Most of the streets were difficult to walk upon and the road I was walking along had trees on both sides that were partly covered by snow. I was enjoying the serene ambience of the old Russian buildings so much that I walked a great distance. But after two hours I wanted to return to the metro station – and realised that I had lost my way. Also my mobile phone battery had run out of power and I was not in a position to use the internet map. So here I was, stranded in those streets and trying my best to look for help, but there were very few people outside on that cold night and the ones whom I met could not speak English. One guy showed me a route to where he thought I wanted to go but, when I followed his advice, I realised that I was heading in the completely wrong direction.

So I started looking for a taxi or a bus station, but could not see any. Most of the signposts were only in the Russian language and I had no idea how to get back to my metro station. It was 11 p.m. already, and I was afraid that I might not be able to make it to the metro in time to catch the last train.

In my heart I was also contemplating why I had decided to come so far, but it was already too late. In life, many times, we experience such feelings but we never get given a second opportunity. I was frustrated, tired and my leather shoes were wet with the snow, when I decided to sit down on a bench for a few minutes to relax and become calm from the inside. After a few minutes I saw a man was walking in my direction, and when he reached me, I asked him for the right direction in English. 'No English, Russian or a little Spanish', he replied. And then I asked him, '¿Tú hablas español?' (Do you speak Spanish?). At this he replied with a smile, 'Sí, sí …' (Yes, yes), 'pero un poco, solo un poco' (But a little, only a little). He had no idea how happy I was in that moment. I introduced myself in Spanish, and explained that as I also knew a little Spanish we could talk in that language because I did not know any Russian. He told me that this way he could also practise his Spanish. Soon we developed a friendship and he told me that he would walk with me to the station because he would not leave me alone in the situation I was in.

He told me that he was married to a Spanish woman

but, as they were now both living in Moscow, he rarely got to practise his Spanish. On that night he was on his post-dinner walk, so he was more than happy to help me reach the metro station. In 30 minutes we arrived at the metro station and the experience was so enlightening that I cannot ask life to give me a lesson in a more practical way than this. And this day I learned that no matter how little knowledge you have, it is not going to be wasted for sooner or later it will be used.

My little knowledge of the Spanish language had helped me to communicate with that Russian man and find my way, and made me realise that my investment in learning a new language was a wise decision and not a waste, as I had been thinking previously.

There is a famous saying by the great writer Oscar Wilde, **'Experience is the one thing you can't get for nothing.'**

You cannot earn experience without going through the maelstrom of life, and without getting lost in it. It is important to get lost sometimes, because only then will you find a new path. You can explore, and create new directions for others to follow. Most people in the world follow what is, for them, the safest route, the one firmly inside their comfort zone. But they keep doing the same things and they end up living a routine life. They also know that they do not enjoy doing the same thing every day, but as they do not have the courage to go against the wave they also do not have the courage to take steps towards their dreams, because they are scared that they will lose their comfort zone.

The journey towards new discoveries and inventions is painful, and those on this path suffer for most of it, but when they succeed, the entire world gathers to hear their stories. These people are just like any of us, but at the same time they are different, and the only difference is that they are ready to experience the undiscovered things in life.

Therefore, go forth and discover on your own. Always remember that you had no choice when you were born. You did not choose your nation or the culture you were brought up in, it just happened. There was no choice, and if there was one then maybe you would have opted for something else. So find your own truth, go on your own journey, and you will definitely find it. Every soul has its own journey and the potential of self-discovery with which to discover this world and the universe.

As a kid I used to ask many questions, and to some of them my father replied, 'You will know once you grow older ...' Maybe I did not like hearing this answer in those moments, but it is true that I did find the answers I wanted with time and experience. I made many mistakes in life and that is how I learned.

Based on this experience I have realised that life is too short and we should not keep waiting for the right time to come. When I see kids and old people sitting inside the park, I always think that these old people were themselves kids one day, but now they are waiting for death. Most people in this world wait for the right time to do things, but the right time never happens. On the day you were born you arrived with limited time (death is inevitable), but the worst thing is that you do not know when the final hour is going to come. At least for products in a shop their expiry date is labelled, but unfortunately this is not the case for humans.

Today I see things differently from the way I used to see them 10 years ago. The same thing will happen to me 10 years down the line from today. Learning should not stop until the last day we spend on earth, and until then we should keep searching and fill our hearts with curiosity. Therefore, never stop yourself from raising questions, because only then will the answers appear. Maybe the answer will appear today, or after a few years or maybe not even in your lifetime, but it is going to happen.

SHANTIH SUTRA 16

Love

This meditation exercise must be practised with a partner. When the opposite sexes (Shiva–Shakti) come together in love, they create new life. For the creation of new life, a male and female energy are required. This exercise is sensitive and sincere, hence it must be practised with a pure heart. Unless you can find the right partner or friend, please never practise this. It must also never be misused for simple sexual favours. The female energy must be respected throughout the exercise, and if at any stage she wants to discontinue she must be allowed to do so, and the same rule applies for the male energy. Unless two souls are compatible and know each other intimately, it must not be practised.

The prerequisite for this exercise is that both persons must already have practised the Vipassana meditation from the previous chapter. Those who have practised 10 days of Vipassana meditation will understand and experience it even more deeply. This exercise is not for sexual pleasure, but for those that have a deep understanding of life and are compassionate towards all living beings, being full of love and peace.

Before starting the exercise below you must both be in a relaxed sitting position and facing each other.

First stage
Breathe in and out 50 times with closed eyes, and then sit silently for one minute.

Breathe in and out 50 times with closed eyes, and then sit silently for two minutes.

Breathe in and out 50 times with closed eyes, and then sit silently for three minutes and then proceed to the next stage.

Second stage: 15 minutes
You must be in a sitting position and facing each other. You should hold each other's hands and breathe in and out slowly together. Create a non-stop loop of breathing together, and experience the breath and the aura of each other. The distance between you should be minimal and you should be physically close enough

to feel each other's energy. You should breathe in and out together for 10 minutes.

Then you should hug each other in a sitting position, and breathe in and out together for five minutes. The separate breaths in and out should fuse into one. There should be no physical and emotional differences left between you.

Physically your two bodies must be together and in relaxing, comfortable and loving position. It should not be artificial, but must come naturally.

Third stage

Look into each other's eyes and say alternately 'I Love You'. The 'I Love You' must have deep meaning and be full of compassion. Here, love is not about lust, but about the respect for the female and male energy. Also experience respect for the universe that blessed two souls to come together in such a way to experience their synergy. Without female energy the male is incomplete, and without male energy the female is likewise weakened. Both energies are equally important and they complement each other. The exercise is sensitive and should be practised with care. If any person feels that their partner is only interested in physical pleasure, then they have every right to quit at this stage. The female energy must always be respected while practising this.

It might be possible that some people will try to misuse this practice just for physical pleasure, but then that is at the discretion of both parties who are going to perform it. It must be an individual decision as to whether you want to practise this exercise or not.

In societies where the genders cannot come together before marriage, this should be only practised between husband and wife. The local culture and social structure must be fully respected.

This exercise is also useful for any couples that are planning to have children. When you make love with full awareness there is a higher probability that your children will be born with more awareness and will be more creative. Your children will always be more compassionate and understanding towards the world.

· · · [17] · · ·

NON-JUDGEMENT

*The ability to observe without evaluating is
the highest form of intelligence.*

Jiddu Krishnamurti

In Tanzania I met a Danish girl who was travelling in East Africa. She told me one day that her parents had never been outside of Denmark, Germany, Netherlands and the UK, and they were worried about visiting India or any African country. When I asked her why this was so, she said 'They keep watching the news on TV, and their knowledge is limited to what they read in the newspapers. They therefore think that India is a primitive place, and that all African countries are having wars and are unsafe.'

So you can see how ignorant this girl's parents were, and how easy it was for them to judge an entire country or a continent. In life it is always easy to judge someone else. We have a tendency to label an entire society based on our personal experiences and prejudices. Even if out of thousands of good experiences one experience goes wrong, we often malign everyone else from that group on the basis of that single incident. We are always in a hurry, always in a rush to judge others and to pass our verdict.

I remember I had some reservations when I received my offer of work in Tanzania, and I started consulting my friends as to whether I should go there. Every one of my Indian friends gave me negative advice. Yet as it turned out, these people had never been to any African countries, and all of their 'advice' was rooted in prejudice. They said to me, 'What's wrong with you? Can't you work in India? Or I suppose if you must go abroad, then why not go to the USA or Europe? Go to a better place than Africa.' But I was also ignorant, because I was seeking advice from friends who had no relevant experience.

For a time this talk deluded my mind and I felt convinced by my friends' arguments, but luckily my heart did not allow me to believe such biased judgement. My heart wanted me to travel the African continent, to see the world through my own eyes and to experience it in reality.

So after pondering the pros and cons for some time, I finally made the decision to travel to Tanzania. And to my surprise, after only a few months I fell in love with this country, and my job allowed me to travel through much of West and Central Africa as well as the East. In the end, I found the continent so beautiful that I stayed there for 20 months. My project was over, but I still did not want to go back to India. I wanted to stay longer, and to explore more. I found that in general, Africans are warm, welcoming, friendly and open people.

But of course I would not have experienced this reality if I had not travelled there. I would have missed out on the entire adventure had I believed those friends, but I took the wise decision to go and experience the truth on my own. Except for a few minor incidents nothing bad happened, and anyway such things happen in every country.

I would like to share my travelling experience of Russia. Before travelling to Russia I had been fed a certain image of this country. The negative, stereotyped image of the old communist state is still favoured by the Western media in relation to Russia, and the way they judge Russian society is biased and inaccurate. The image we are fed is that of an authoritarian leadership, military dominance, and the suppression of personal freedom, but when I travelled to Moscow and St Petersburg I found this country to be completely the opposite. It broke many of the myths that I had been programmed with. The first myth was that in cold countries, in general, people are cold in behaviour, but that was not the case in Russia. People were instead warm, friendly and willing to help me around. The temperature was close to zero degrees when I was travelling there, but still the warmth inside the hearts of ordinary Russians was amazing.

The social behaviour was very much like in any Western country. To my surprise I saw fewer homeless people in Russian cities than in the UK. While talking to locals, they expressed their dismay about endemic corruption but otherwise they looked as happy as any Westerner might be with their own government. At the same time, however, a few people complained that there was not so much freedom in the media as you can enjoy in a Western style democracy. But then again it is true that many Western democracies today are also suffering from unprecedented state suppression of freedom, and political corruption. Undoubtedly what exists in Russia is not a decentralised system of power, but each sociopolitical system has its own drawbacks and to an extent it also caters to local social needs and historical experience. And unless we have different types of social and political systems, we will never be able to compare the pros and cons of each other; and that is why we should not try to paint the entire world with the same colour.

If I had not travelled to Russia, and had restricted my knowledge only to the Western media's stereotypical views, then I was not going to experience the positive side of this society.

The same thing happened to me before travelling to Europe. In this case, a few Indians who had returned to India after working a few years in Europe told me that I would not be welcome in Europe, that it was hard to make friends there, and that Europeans lived in a closed community. Even a few European friends in Tanzania told me the same thing, namely that as an Asian I might face challenges. But when I went backpacking for a month across six European countries, I found that the people were welcoming, friendly and caring. I met friends and found hosts in these countries. In fact I have always found friends everywhere, and have made friends quickly. In my experience it all depends on how you see the world and on how open you are to it. In essence, it all depends on how much love you have in your heart.

I remember that one evening I was sitting in The Trinity Bar in Dar-Es-Salaam, Tanzania, and I heard someone say, 'I hate Indians.' I turned round and saw the girl who had just said these words. I knew her. She noticed me staring and tried to make politically correct excuses in an embarrassing, awkward manner. Never be too fast in rushing to judgement. It is easy to label someone. Your experiences are always of individuals and in addition these are filtered through your own cultural consciousness; therefore, based upon your own limited experience it is simply not fair to put preconceived notions into your head and to spread unwarranted negativity.

If today some shoot-out happens in the USA and a

black man is murdered by the police, the entire world starts accusing the USA of being a racist society – but we have forgotten that this country, twice in a row, elected a man as a president who was of African origin.

Again, after the demolition of the Babri Masjid mosque, the world started saying that India was not a safe place for Muslims. The entire Indian society was suddenly labelled 'communalist', and everyone forgot its many thousands of years of multicultural unity and spiritual heritage.

I would like to share one experience, about the way that I experienced the lessons of judgement and non-judgement at two different airports.

Once, after undergoing all the checks and security clearances, I was standing in a queue waiting to board a plane for Istanbul at Bristol Airport in the UK. Then, out of the blue, a security officer came to me and asked, 'Sir, would you mind coming with me for a few minutes?' This officer was in uniform, and I think that he was from the UK Home Office. I followed him, and he took me aside into a corner.

'May I know where you are going?' he asked me.

'I'm going to Istanbul', I replied. But then I remembered that there was a bit more to the story, so I quickly added that it was only a one-day stop-over in Istanbul, and that after that I would go on to New Delhi.

'Ok, and may I know what you do in UK?' he continued.

So I told him that I worked for a telecom company and I gave him its name.

'Hmm. Do you have a valid visa to work in UK?' was his next question. This question was not required at all, because you cannot work in the UK for telecom companies unless you have a valid UK work permit, and this is especially true for a non-European.

'Yes, of course,' I replied, 'I've been more than eight months working here and now I'm going on my holidays. I can show you the work permit stamped on my passport.'

He spent some time studying this and then added, 'I believe you will spend more time in Istanbul. Are you carrying enough cash to do this?'

By this time I was very annoyed, and told him that I had a credit and debit card and 600 rupees in cash. After giving him that information he concluded the interview, even though if he had been doing his 'security' job properly he would have realised that 600 Indian rupees hardly equals £6–7, and what can you do with so little money in Istanbul? Shortly I rejoined the queue and boarded the flight. Everyone standing in the queue was looking at me and wondering what had been going on, so the whole experience was not comfortable.

Later, I observed that I was the only brown-skinned man in the whole queue. It might be possible that this officer became suspicious just because I was from Asia, and that is why he took me aside and asked me all those questions. With those illogical questions that were not required, I thought that maybe he was testing me and trying to find some cracks in my explanation in order to exploit them. But this did not only happen to me in the UK.

Later, when I travelled to Russia, I experienced something more serious than this. When I arrived at

Moscow airport from Zurich, as per routine, I showed up at the emigration counter to get my passport stamped. The lady looked at me and at my passport multiple times and then asked, 'Where you come from?' I told her that I was coming from London with a stop-over in Zurich. On this she asked, 'Why Moscow?' I explained to her politely that I was there on holiday but she was not convinced. She started turning the pages of my passport and called someone on the phone. Later, two people in uniform came and asked me to follow them. By now I was a little bit suspicious about what was going on. The uniformed men requested that I sit in a small dingy room and left me. When I sat down and looked up, I found that a CCTV camera was above my head and looking at me with an eagle's eye. The room had just the one bench where I was sitting.

I laid my jacket out on the bench and took out my mobile phone to check the time. I was sitting calmly, but at the same time my mind was racing. The first thing that came to my mind was that this was the first time I was in Russia and I did not know what would happen or why they were treating me in this way. The second thought was how to reach out to my family and friends from there if they did not let me go.

At the same time I was coming from the UK and the current relationship between the UK and Russia was not amicable, so that could be also one of the potential reasons to question me more. But no matter what thoughts were coming into my mind, I had no clue what would happen next.

After 15–20 minutes a new guy arrived and asked

me, 'Why you have two passports?' I explained to him that one of the passports was an old one and another one was new – but since the old one had some valid visa stamps, I always carried both. Then he threw me another question. 'You are from India, but coming from London?' he raised his eyebrow in suspicion. 'Yes Sir, I work in the UK, but I am an Indian citizen', I replied. He then asked me how long I would stay in Russia, and I said that I was on holiday there for 10 days.

'Please come with me', he asked. I stood up, retrieved my jacket and followed him. He then took me back to the same emigration counter, and told the lady who had initiated the whole process something in Russian. Now this same lady scanned all my European visa stamps, and that was quite unsettling because I had never seen anything like this in the past, but finally she stamped my passport and let me leave the airport.

These two experiences at the airport could be perceived from different angles. One way to see it is that because I am an Asian, and in both cases I was in a minority, security personnel asked more questions to ensure they were only letting the right person, with valid documents, enter their country. These might be the instructions given to them, but at the same time it also shows that in the current world many systems have become more judgemental than before and are starting to target people, who appear to come from a specific community, in an organised manner.

But holistically, by not judging someone you can do yourself a favour, and you will have less bitterness towards anyone. Therefore it is important to analyse things rationally, and to accept that life is subjective and not objective.

Evil is present in every society, race and faith. And we should not forget that we all belong to the same species, and this is called Humanity. We all walk on two legs, breathe in the same manner and biologically we are all the same. The only way you can become 'better' is by practising peace, spreading love and becoming wise. Otherwise there is no way to prove that you are better than the rest.

I would like to share an incident that happened to me when I was travelling in Slovakia in January 2014. I was standing outside Bratislava train station with a friend, busy taking pictures, when suddenly I heard someone shout, 'Do not take my picture!' When I looked at the source, I saw a man of African origin was looking angrily at me. I was taking pictures in a completely different direction, so technically it was impossible for me to take his picture. I ignored him and after a minute he came over to me and asked angrily, 'Are you from India?' I replied in the affirmative and on hearing this he replied violently, 'All Indians must be killed!' I could not understand why he said this, but I found him violent and his statement shocking. Trying to ignore him, I started talking to my friend. Later he returned and this time he shouted at me, 'You Indians beat up Nigerians in India. You must be beaten everywhere, you must be wiped from the earth. What are you doing here?' And at last I understood the back-story behind his rant. A few months previously, two Nigerian students in New

Delhi had been assaulted by commuters in a metro station, and this news had spread everywhere through social media. They were beaten by the public on the assumption that they were 'misbehaving with girls'. Nobody should take the law into their own hands like that and the video of the Delhi crowd beating the Nigerian students was deplorable – no sane person would support such a barbaric act.

But this Nigerian man living far away from his own country had developed a serious hatred against the entire nation of India. So he saw me, and immediately started venting his anger. I controlled myself, because I knew that this man was ignorant and there was no point in having a verbal duel with him.

There is a famous saying, 'An eye for an eye only ends up making the whole world blind.' Therefore, my friend and I decided to leave that place and went inside the train station. But the experience made me realise that an ignorant judgement is a highly dangerous decision, and that it hurts everyone to no end.

Do not be in a hurry to judge, even if you experience something that seems to be wrong. It is often either a problem related to that one individual, or maybe you failed to understand that person and you need to go deeper inside your heart and analyse the situation in a compassionate manner.

SHANTIH SUTRA 17

Observe Children, or Birds and Animals

First stage
Breathe in and out 50 times with closed eyes, and then sit silently for one minute.

Breathe in and out 50 times with closed eyes, and then sit silently for two minutes and then proceed to the next stage.

Second stage: 10 minutes
Sit silently with closed eyes, and then proceed to the next stage.

Third stage: 30 minutes

If you have a child, observe every movement they make and respond to their every move or question. They are relatively new to this world and everything is fresh for them. Their minds are very curious and they are keen to observe new things. When they are playing or talking – listen to their noise, their playfulness and freedom. Observe their innocence and imagine that you are also newly born, and ready to open your mind and heart to new things. Reflect on yourself through this exercise, and in such a way try to become non-judgemental in your own life.

If you do not have any children of your own, you can spend time with the children of your friends or relatives.

This technique is about observing the innocence and openness of children. Preferably practise this with children that are not more than three years old – the younger they are, the more effective the exercise is.

Or if you do not have an opportunity to spend time with children, then you can practise the same exercise while watching birds and animals. Birds and animals are completely in their own world and are very much at peace. Practise only with herbivorous animals and not with birds or animals that are potentially violent. Likewise the creatures under study should not be caged or kept inside a zoo. They must be free in the same way that we are free in our world.

· · · [18] · · ·

THE IMPORTANCE OF DEATH

As a well spent day brings happy sleep, so life well used brings happy death.

Leonardo Da Vinci

On the seashore the children were playing with sand and busy building pyramids, tunnels and castles. The sun was going down and their parents shouted from afar, 'It's time to go home – it's already late, let's go.' So the children left things as they were and ran off towards their parents, leaving those half-finished castles, tunnels and pyramids behind on the sand.

At the age of 18, and under the suspicion of having a rare type of cancer, I was hospitalised for two nights at an Army Research and Referral centre in New Delhi. Suddenly, for the first time ever, I felt I was hovering between life and death. In life we never know how things are going to turn out, but deep in my mind and heart I felt confident that nothing bad would happen. On the morning of the first day I had an appointment with the head of the oncology department, and in the army he held the rank of major-general. He was a Sikh, a tall man with a strong physique. When I met him, he asked me a few basic questions about whether I smoked or drank etc. But I was neither smoking nor drinking at that age. He explained that they would perform a minor operation and after analysing the data they would make a decision about whether to keep me hospitalised, or to discharge me.

My report was going to come the next day, so there was 24 hours of waiting. When I returned to my ward, I saw many patients who were in the last stages of their lives and they knew very well that they were going to die, as they had already gone through chemotherapy many times with no success. Their heads were either completely shaved or maybe they had lost their hair, and most of them had mouth cancer. Many of them had a food pipe fitted into their necks. I remember how one middle-aged military man came and sat close to me and asked me a question by waving his finger. I think it meant, 'What happened to you?' I explained my situation to him and he replied by writing on a piece of paper. 'You are young, so I hope that nothing bad happens to you. I pray to God. We are all here in the final stage of cancer. I am not going to live – the doctors have already told me.' His note was sad. I spent that day looking at those patients and looking through the window at the bustling life outside. I was looking at kids who were playing, young men walking fast on the street, cars passing by and at people coming into or going out of the hospital. And then I was looking at the patients lying on their beds, counting the dwindling number of days left in their lives. The experience was enlightening; something deep inside me happened at that moment. In a moment of transformation I realised that the gap between life and death is thin, and until you come close to death you never realise the full importance of life. How important it is to live life meaningfully and deeply, because once you die there is no return!

That night I lay in bed, waiting for the next day when my results would come through. Where I had been so sure before, there was now anxiety in my head. I was restless, and I was dreading any bad news. At the age of 18, no one expects to suffer horribly and die. Fortunately, when I was summoned once again before the Sikh doctor, the data was fine. There was no cancer, and I was advised to go for some laser treatment only.

But those two days at the hospital gave me a powerful understanding of life and death.

Death is inevitable. Anyone who is born is going to die one day. It is the biggest truth of this world, that nothing is here permanently, but still we keep on deluding ourselves and avoiding the fact that one day we are going to leave everything behind. Even the body that we care for 24 hours a day is not going to be with us, never mind our other materialistic possessions. Deep inside we know full well that death will come for us one day, but we do not want to think about it and so we try to avoid this thought as much as possible. We think it is 'negative' to think about death, simply because when it happens, it will happen, so there's no point in thinking about it. But the point here is not to think about death in a negative, fearful way, or by becoming sad and ceasing to enjoy the present moment.

The point is instead to become aware of our day-to-day life, and keep in mind that since death is inevitable we should try to focus on what we are really doing in life, who we are, and in what direction we are travelling. It is important to have a deeper purpose in life, to be more aware from the inside and to be more sensitive towards society and humanity, becoming more aware of nature and our surroundings, and start contributing before it is too late. If we live with full awareness that one day we have to die and leave everything behind, we can become more realistic in our lives. Maybe we will realise how important life is and that we should not waste it on frivolous distractions.

Most of us spend our entire lives chasing our desires for money, fame, power, sex, material things, etc. We keep ourselves busy until the day that death suddenly arrives. It appears as disconcertingly as an uninvited guest; a surprise visitor because no one is prepared, no one wants to see it, but the party is suddenly over and everything ends. When it happens, most of our desires are left unfinished and in those last moments it leaves a big emptiness inside our heart and soul. The soul leaves the body, and remains restless with the thought that life is over and it could not finish the many things that were supposed to be achieved. But unfortunately, there is no opportunity left to go back to the same human body and the same life.

That is why death is at the centre of all religions. There is a big emphasis on coming to terms with death and most theologies and moral principles are built around it. There are a few basic principles that are common to all religions. Every religion talks about some form of karma, and based on your karma comes your afterlife journey – to Heaven or Hell, or to rebirth.

Death is the end of an old life and beginning of a new journey. If you follow major religions like Christianity and Islam, your present life is considered to be your only opportunity and after this you have your day of judgement. These religions do not believe in rebirth, so your post-death journey is decided by the karmic actions you took in your one life.

But in other major religions like Hinduism and Buddhism death is just an opportunity for a new birth, and once you have reached salvation then you have the choice after death as to whether you want to be reborn again or not. But once again, everything is based on the karmic actions that you performed when you were alive.

These basic principles are common to all the world's religions.

As the post-life journey of the soul is common to all religions, should we not try to do something meaningful with our present lives? Why not share our love, happiness, wisdom, good health and wealth with others, and be kind towards humanity so that our end should be peaceful and content?

We should invest in knowledge, wisdom and in strengthening our character instead of running on the treadmill of anxiety over short-term objectives. We should invest instead in the wisdom that we will carry on with us even after the body dies.

SHANTIH SUTRA 18

Attend a Funeral

We should experience life and death closely, or we will not be able to appreciate the importance of both. We should follow a path that most are scared of and will not follow. To fully experience life, you also have to experience death in a beautiful way. No matter how awkward or frightening it may look, just gather yourself enough courage, have a positive mindset and follow the steps below with complete faith.

First stage
Breathe in and out 30 times with closed eyes, and then sit silently for one minute.

Breathe in and out 30 times with closed eyes, and then sit silently for two minutes.

Breathe in and out 30 times with closed eyes, and then sit silently for three minutes and then proceed to the next stage.

In the entire process please keep your eyes closed and you should be sitting somewhere on the floor, on the ground or a flat surface to feel comfortable. While sitting, your back must be straight but the rest of your body should be in a relaxed position. You should not become stiff, so you should sit up straight with your arms resting on your knees.

If you are feeling sick and cannot sit, you can do this while lying on the bed. Follow the same instructions – but if you are too ill then do not practise it; please respect your body and make your decision based on your body's energy. If your body does not allow you, then simply avoid this exercise and practise later when you feel more energetic.

Second stage: 15 minutes
Close your eyes and let all kinds of thoughts enter your head. Keep them flowing as they happen in the moment, but this time you have to watch them from far away. Watch all your thoughts like you watch a movie or look at a painting. Keep watching your thoughts but just do not be a part of them. You only have to be a witness to your thoughts. If your thoughts make you smile, smile, and if they make you sad, become sad, and after watching the games of your mind for 15 minutes, try to stop your mind from

thinking. Try to focus on the spot between your two eyes and become focused on nothing else.

Third stage: 15 minutes

For the next 15 minutes you should close the doors of your mind to any thoughts that enter, but do not struggle or waste too much energy if your mind is still wandering and thoughts are flowing.

Fourth stage: 60 minutes

Visit a graveyard or crematorium, and observe this place closely and silently. Sit in a corner and see all those tombs or memorials, and also the people who are visiting to perform rituals. This exercise will remind you that one day you also have to leave this world, so you should not take things for granted and should resolve to the best of your ability to finish your work, wishes and goals before the time comes. You must also understand that in the past these dead people were also alive like you, but today they are no more. This exercise will help you to detach yourself from materialistic pursuits and refresh your mind and soul with more meaningful and deep thoughts.

You do not have to become sad while observing this – the purpose is to go inward in self-introspection and to observe the gap between life and death. The exercise is very powerful if you do it with complete awareness. Death can be a beautiful phase in the human journey if it happens with awareness. And this will only happen when you detach from the materialistic things that you encounter while living in this world.

Spend at least one hour or more sitting in this place as you reflect on life, death, and your own karmic journey.

RELIGION AND FAITH

There is no need for temples, no need for complicated philosophies. My brain and my heart are my temples; my philosophy is kindness.

Tenzin Gyatso, 14th Dalai Lama

A German friend who visited me in Bristol, UK, once told me a strange tale: 'Chit, today when I was walking alone in the city centre, this guy approached me and said "Do you have a problem with your leg?" First of all I was surprised that a stranger was coming up to me and asking this, but before I could answer he followed that up with another question. "Are you from Germany?" I smiled and replied, "Yes, I am from Germany. But why are you asking?" He smiled and started talking to me. I explained to him that I was visiting Bristol and staying with a friend, and then suddenly he told me, "You had a problem with your left ankle and have had an operation." Once again he freaked me out, because I had not shared this news with anyone in Bristol and had met him only five minutes earlier. "Yes, I had surgery last year, but how come you know about this?" He smiled and advised me, "You should start going to church again," and then he left me alone.'

My friend told me that she will never forget this experience and that it was surreal. But I listened to her gladly and completely believed in her. Because personally I have come across many mystics in my life, so I have to accept and listen to such things. While travelling, I met random people who told me things that were surreal and unbelievable, but those predictions later became a reality. In every part of the world there are mystics or visionaries who can see what a normal human being cannot see or experience. Ever since I acquired a keen interest in religious studies and learned to explore different religions, I have come across people everywhere with a mystical depth that rational people cannot explain away through logical explanation and reasoning.

The great importance of religion in life is that it gives us discipline and helps us to realise every day that we are not only born to eat, sleep, give birth to kids and die one day. Life is far more important than this, and there are far more meaningful things to do before death occurs.

But at the same time each religion has boundaries and many pitfalls – if you are part of a religious system that was created hundreds of years ago, with stringent rules that were relevant at that time (but not anymore), then it will create conflict around you if you are trying to practise all those rules blindly. A religion places rules and regulations on its congregation just like a parliament enforces policies on its nation. Unless the parliament enforces its rules, it will not be able to contribute towards its nation's development. The rules of a parliament are, however, limited to a single country, but that is not true for a religion and the conflicts caused by a religion and its followers are much larger and affect many nations.

Each religion is encumbered by umpteen flaws and fables and therefore you should not believe in everything it says. So yes, sometimes you do have to be rational. Beneath all the 'truths' you get told to believe in that are just made-up stories, in essence every religion preaches the same love, peace and humanity – but when its followers take their own beliefs so seriously that they reject the others' beliefs and create confrontations, sometimes this leads to religious wars, death, and devastation.

The dilemma of this world is that it is difficult to ignore religion, but at the same time it is not pragmatic enough to make it the centre of your life. So if we stop following religious books and their supposed rules myopically and fanatically, then their wisdom might help us to be more in harmony with our present lives.

The irony is that all the great religious figures and founders came up with new ideas and philosophies that criticised the existing religious practices and tried to bring reforms in their society, but unfortunately, in time, their followers became dogmatic and rigid about their master's teachings. Over time, each religion became conjoined in some form with the political world and it was in the interests of its guardians to infringe upon daily life through ever-stricter laws. Therefore, every teacher set out against the existing beliefs of the religion of his day, but his followers simply created a new dogmatism in his name. This is because, regardless of what the actual teachings have to say, there is always plenty of power politics circulating around religious institutions, and the people who desire to control such institutions. The powerful priests, preachers, popes, and mullahs know well that unless they give prominence to one book, person, constitution and to one religious body, it will become difficult to control and rule the religion's followers. Therefore they continue to reinterpret the rules, regulations and foundation myths, and by enshrining these in dogma they seek to exploit and rule the community at large.

It is of course true that many things in this world and life are beyond logical reasoning and its demonstrable proofs, so the only way to experience such things is to first of all react spontaneously to them and perhaps later, in a reflective mode, we might discover something meaningful. We need to find a balance between faith and the logical mind, because a society based only on faith can lead to destruction. If you have the belief that only your faith is the best and only way to experience salvation or the higher truth, then you are absolutely wrong. And if you practise this bigotry in your daily life then you will obviously experience clashes, because there are so many people living on earth who have reasons to believe that their faith is better.

The question is – is there a way to find a balance between life and religion, and the world in which we live? Is there a way to make people accept the fact that it is good to believe in your own theology, but it is also great to give freedom and respect to other peoples' theologies?

The answer is that this will not happen until we start reading about other faiths and start visiting their sacred sites.

During my master's degree course in computer science at Hamdard University, New Delhi, I had many Syrian classmates and one day while discussing books by spiritual philosophers I advised one of my friends to read a book. 'Fouad, you should read this book, I am sure you will learn many new things through its teachings.' My Syrian friend looked worried: 'Yes, that certainly sounds like a really interesting philosopher, but can you tell me his religious background?' he asked me.

'He was born into a Jainist family,' I replied, 'but he was open-minded and spoke about the varying strengths that the world's different religions all had.' On hearing this, my friend shook his head sadly. 'Sorry Chit, but my religion doesn't allow me to read the philosophers of another religion.' So I left the conversation there, but I felt bad for him because by living under such rigid boundaries he was missing opportunities to grow as a person.

I always had serious doubts about any religion that would proscribe its followers from reading books of wisdom written by people from different faiths. Even if your religion says this, you should not follow it; it is simple – nobody can legitimately stop you from reading. Surely it must only be you who is closed-minded and not ready to read. If you are born and brought up in a conservative religious country, then we can readily understand that you will not find books from other religions there, but if you are travelling and studying in a different country then you have every opportunity to enquire into different faiths, or at least listen to them and see what they are talking about, and find out how much we can learn from them.

So I felt bad for my classmate that he had missed an opportunity to read works by other writers and philosophers, because by doing this he was only harming himself and also creating a negative image about his own religious community. Just imagine if he practised the same principles before going to buy a book on computer science! Say if he had started reading only those science books written by Muslim scholars and rejected all the books written by other writers, then what kind of computer engineer would he have become?

When I was a student in Hamdard University and I was coming out of a Friday namaaz (prayers) with a few friends at the local mosque, one of these friends advised me, 'Chit, now that you've started doing what a Muslim does, why do not you convert to Islam?' I stopped and looked at him. 'But what will change inside if I change my religion and outer appearance?' I replied politely. On hearing this response, the rest of my Muslim friends nodded in agreement with me. By simply converting people to a certain religion, nothing much is going to change inside for them. It is like if you keep changing your clothes to suit the occasion, but inside you are the same person. By wearing different clothes you can change appearance for a time and may also feel happy, but once again, in time, you will start to experience the same kind of emotions that propelled you to change them in the first place. Similarly, unless something deep first changes inside you, nothing will change by blindly following a new religion. The focus should be on learning constantly through each other, and this can only happen when we open our hearts and minds and do not get stuck with following rituals.

Society will flourish only when Hindus start reading Christian books and Christians read Muslim books, and Muslims read Hindu and Buddhist books. And in such a way we all could start by reading books from different religions, and if we find something better we could start practising it in daily life – and in this way we will be able to understand each other in much better ways.

And we should do this in the same way as when we study in a school – we never question a mathematics book just because it is written by, say, a Christian or a Jewish writer, so in the same way we should be open to learn from people born into different faiths.

When we are sick, we listen to the advice of a doctor and take the medicine prescribed. We do so blindly without thinking about which faith he comes from, so in the same way we should be ready to learn different philosophies no matter from where it comes. If a wise person says something, it is important to listen to him or her no matter where they come from.

This earth has too many religions already and we do not need any more. There is enough religious extremism in this world and Mother Earth cannot take any more. Religious fanatics of all faiths are destroying many lives and even honest, ordinary followers are responsible because they do not question the self-appointed leaders of their faith. They should either start to leave the faith or else strongly question its practices, otherwise, they will keep silently allowing such atrocities to spread across the world and in so doing provoke others to become judgemental against them, and this applies to every religion.

It is the responsibility of every religious follower to question their faith's leaders and try to think rationally, or otherwise, they will be the ones responsible for helping religious extremism to grow.

Religious reforms are very important after a certain point because religion does not limit itself to preaching peace and love – it starts teaching you what to wear, how to dress, what to eat, how many times to worship, and starts preaching thousands of rules to be practised in your life otherwise something bad will happen after death – and this creates misconceptions in many minds; that is why all religions should be constantly evolving through reform.

No matter how much you try to avoid religious discussion or debate, its impact on daily life, and the spiritual influence and the conditioning it imparts, is still strong in most peoples' psyches. While travelling across the USA, Germany, Spain, Hungary, England, Kenya, Russia, and Chad, I have been questioned on many different occasions about my religious beliefs. People were always curious to know what faith I practised, and what my religious identity was. Even though I had often just met them first time, they were still curious to know about my religious background.

As I said in the beginning that we seem to need religion, at the same time we have to be rational enough to make our own decisions about what should be followed or not. This is going to be subjective and every choice is an individual decision, but in simple words if you become aware that your religion denies you the freedom to explore other faiths, then it is evident that you are on the wrong journey and that you should choose your own path.

The only possible way to make this earth a better place to live is to start respecting all faiths – whether these are Hinduism, Buddhism, Jainism, Christianity, Islam, Judaism, Zoroastrianism, Sikhism, Bahai, etc.

SHANTIH SUTRA 19

Visit a Church, Temple, Mosque or Monastery

First stage
Breathe in and out 50 times with closed eyes, and then wait for one minute.

Breathe in and out 50 times with closed eyes, and then wait for one minute and move to second stage.

Second stage
Visit a church, temple, mosque or monastery, but this building must not be from your own faith. For example, if you are a Christian perhaps visit a temple or if you are a Hindu maybe visit a mosque, or if you are a Muslim you might visit a church.

'I love you when you bow in your mosque, kneel in your temple, pray in your church. For you and I are sons of one religion, and it is the spirit.' – Khalil Gibran

I have personally experienced peace whenever I visited a mosque, a church or a temple. And I also find peace when I sit alone and meditate, because peace is inside me and nowhere else.

I always wondered why so much importance is given to churches, temples or mosques, and why people of wisdom insisted that we should visit these places. I think the reason is deeper than it looks. During my travels, whenever I found a church, I entered inside and by sitting there for a few minutes alone I found peace. For a few moments I forgot everything around me and connected directly with my soul. I practised this many times while travelling in Europe. And I did the same thing in mosques while travelling in Africa, and again in the temples of India.

Many atheists say that there is no point in visiting these places and you can achieve this state just by sitting in your home or in a field. They have a point, and up to certain level I agree with them, but then again I differ from them because if you create a place where everyone is coming to seek peace, then that place will have a strong energy. That place will have a different type of vibration that cannot be matched by any other place. That is why when you go to visit such places, their energy suddenly hits you. You feel deeply connected to your inner self, and for a few seconds you forget mundane things. These places of worship make you to forget your ego, to kneel your body and touch the feet of spiritual figures.

If you go deep, you will discover that the prayers in Islam, Christianity and Hinduism are all meditative exercises. They work similarly to meditation, allowing you to sit alone and practise your inner peace. And when you pray in a group, the positive energy of each individual starts working together and you achieve the result sooner.

Because of these reasons, visits to these places were written in religious books and were recommended by the religion; so at least out of fear of God or Heaven or Hell, people were forced to visit. There could be an argument that there is no point when things are forced upon you. But it is also true that it is just like a mother feeding her baby with milk, and the baby is resisting, yet the mother knows that her child needs this to gain strength and grow bigger. In the same way, during the initial stages of spiritual self-discovery you may need to visit such places, but once you are able to realise your own truth these things become secondary; however, such a journey takes time.

The famous boxing champion Muhammad Ali said, 'Rivers, ponds, lakes and streams – they all have different names, but they all contain water.' In the same way religions also have different names – but they all contain spiritual truths.

No matter which religious practice you follow, or where you go for worship, its purpose is the same. The truth you seek is your own discovery of peace, love and humanity. The forms taken might be different, the rituals might be different, but the purpose is the same. When you listen to good music it makes you happy, but this music could be in any language or from any origin. At the bottom of the heart, the basic human pulse is always the same.

· · · [20] · · ·

SPIRITUALITY AND AWARENESS

Just as a candle cannot burn without fire,
men cannot live without a spiritual life.

Mahatma Buddha

The Prophet was angry and he said, 'I never imagined that I would see Muslims killing each other in the name of Jihad, Shia, and Sunni. I believed reforms would take place with time.' Next to him, Christ put down his glass of wine and replied, 'Well, for my part, I too never imagined that what I taught would produce Orthodox, Protestants, Catholics …' Krishna then passed by looking for his flute, but he stopped for a few seconds to join the conversation, saying, 'You think that's bad? Let me tell you how shameful it is to see Hindus so obsessed with caste.' Finally Buddha, who was sitting in the lotus position on the floor, opened his eyes and said, 'At least we tried, and I'm quite sure others will keep trying after us.'

When you move beyond artificial religious boundaries, starting to experience your own truth and choosing your own way, it means that you are following a spiritual path. Your spiritual path is the inward journey you take once you start believing in things only because you have experienced them – it is completely experience-based. Even though you cannot explain your experiences to the outer world in terms of rational thinking, you still feel and experience it. Spirituality is also based on faith, but this way, you have your own faith that is personal and very much based on experience. This faith is not ascribed by the society or religious community where you grew up; instead, it is completely based on your own journey and whatever you discovered while travelling across the face of the earth.

The spiritual path is deep and liberates you from

the dogmas of this society. It liberates you from the conditionings of religion, race, class and caste.

Spirituality teaches you that there is no 'Ultimate Truth', but there is 'A Truth', and every person has their own interpretation of it. Spirituality helps you to realise that human civilisation is always evolving, and likewise its beliefs and faiths. There is nothing permanent on this earth, and in comparison to the vastness of the universe even our understanding of 'truth' is relatively minuscule, so there is no need to follow any belief too seriously. There is certainly no need to become fanatical about any one philosophy, and we should never try to enforce our choice onto others. Being spiritual means to keep practising with constant evolution and to keep learning – learning from different cultures, civilisations, faiths and societies, and also through our own experience. Nobody knows the actual truth, and 'truth' is so subjective anyway that it should never be enforced on anyone.

Even the concept of gods or goddesses looks childish when we look at the complexity and vastness of this universe. So far we haven't even fully explored our own solar system, and we know that there are billions of galaxies out there, and therefore billions of planets, so who knows how many millions of other life forms there are? The reach of science and so-called scientific advancement is limited, so just as with religion our current understanding of science also has its limitations. And the only way to expand our knowledge is to allow spirituality and science to both keep evolving non-stop and grow together. Since we don't know what is happening on other planets and as we don't have proof to convince ourselves that there is anything beyond what we can see, then how can we believe blindly in everything we have been taught by our religious and scientific leaders?

The fact is that everything has limitations, and just like everybody has their limits of imagination, in the same way each society and religious structure has its own limitations. We can only overcome this once we start experiencing things on our own, when we allow ourselves and others to go on different paths, and when we no longer believe in something just because it is either written somewhere or was said by some famous person. We have to understand that each great religious figure has his or her own limitations, and their prophecies or teachings were limited by their time and cultural context. We should definitely listen to or read their works, however, and if possible extract whatever knowledge is relevant to ourselves, because we cannot ignore the fact that a few human beings are ahead of the rest of us, and they have more wisdom and depth of thought to share with others.

Spirituality makes you wiser and gives you wisdom. And wisdom can only be achieved through experience, and you can only go through different experiences when you allow yourself to experience life. The goal of life should be to attain wisdom, and there is no end to it, for you will keep becoming wiser and wiser with each passing year and even beyond your physical body (after death). Wisdom is not a position or a fixed destination, it is an endless journey and the deeper you go, the deeper you want to dive.

Spirituality makes you aware, as awareness and

wisdom are interrelated, and you cannot separate them. The wiser you become, the more aware you become in life. You cannot simply become aware through formal education, although it helps to a certain extent, and to become aware you need to work on enriching your soul and attaining wisdom. This can only happen when you open your heart and mind to accept different faiths and the research of scientific investigations. This awareness is the most important element in life and every human must strive to become more and more aware with each passing day.

There is no end to the mysteries of the galaxies, and in the same way there should be no limitations to our spiritual awareness. We all should keep trying our best to learn and experience more, and then to share it with others.

SHANTIH SUTRA 20

Regression Therapy

First stage
Breathe in and out 50 times with closed eyes, and
wait for one minute.
　　Breathe in and out 50 times with closed eyes, and
wait for one minute.

Second stage: 10 minutes
Sit silently with closed eyes, and then proceed to the
next stage.

Third stage: 15 minutes
With your eyes still closed, revisit your darkest expe-

rience and try to re-imagine it in the present moment. This should be the ugliest event in your life that still haunts you and scares you every day. Try to relive the moment with the intention that you do not ever want to see it again, or for that matter wish for anyone else to go through it.

You have to truly relive that moment, but very slowly. This time you have the freedom to replay that real-life moment at the speed you want. When it happened you had no idea how to handle the situation, but now you have the freedom to visualise it again and to replay it in your mind under the control of your own will. The darkest moment that is stuck in your mind must now go slowly out of your life, and it will happen only once you start revisiting it with a different approach and this time with more patience, awareness and compassion.

Fourth Stage: 30 minutes

You have to write on a piece of paper about that darkest moment for 30 minutes. You have to let go of that past through your writings. While writing, you don't have to focus on grammar, punctuation and creativity. You just need to keep writing non-stop in the language you are comfortable. If you think 30 minutes are not enough, take more time to write. At the end of this exercise read through what you have written and if you wish, please destroy this paper.

You may need to repeat this exercise many times, but you should only repeat the regression for as long as it takes for you to fully transcend your negative life experience.

Most of the time bad events occur very suddenly, and they surprise us and make us panic because we had never imagined ourselves facing that kind of situation. But if you are aware that you are going to enter the darkness you will be prepared for the light on the other side, and you will not be so scared. Then you can face the darkness much easier.

When you practise this it might be possible that you start crying. If this happens then it is good, so there is no need to be worried. Let the tears come, and with them your dark past has a chance to go out too. It will take some time to move beyond this type of memory, but it is absolutely possible to move away from the sadness or torment you feel on a permanent basis.

You have to do this entire process with closed eyes, except the writing part, sitting alone somewhere inside your house or a garden.

If possible, do this exercise many times in life until you free yourself completely from that negative past experience.

· · · [21] · · ·

ENLIGHTENMENT

Knowing others is wisdom, knowing
yourself is Enlightenment.

Lao Tzu

When a mystic finally attained enlightenment after a decade-long struggle, he started gathering listeners from around the world. His words of wisdom reached far and wide and he gathered many followers. Once he was asked by an ardent student, 'How did you feel in those days of struggle, and what was the key that led you to attaining wisdom?' On hearing this, he asked his disciple to block her nose with fingers and stop breathing completely. So she did as directed, but after only a minute or two she had to start breathing again. Then the master asked her, 'How did you feel in that moment?'. She thought for a moment before replying. 'Total suffocation and restlessness', she said.

The master now gave his answer, 'That's the key to enlightenment and success towards any goal, and that's also how I felt until the time that I attained Nirvana (Samadhi). You will need dedication and patience on this journey.'

Enlightenment is not some 'destination' that you attain where you become free from all worldly ills and problems, or a place where you start behaving in an entirely new and 'enlightened' way.

It does not mean that all worldly desires and fears disappear. An enlightened person will still experience ecstasy, anxiety, fear and pleasure. An enlightened person will still be attracted to beautiful faces or delicious food, and they might just as easily experience disappointment when things go terribly wrong. There is a false notion about enlightened people that infers that once you become enlightened, then you magically move away from worldly issues and simultaneously find a solution to all of your problems. Such a misunderstanding implies that you will never get angry, never feel disappointed, never experience nervousness, and that you move away completely from all worldly desires; but that is simply not true.

Yet undoubtedly, an enlightened person's approach to the world does change in a positive way – for instead of reacting, an enlightened person starts acting. Normally, if something goes terribly wrong and against someone's wishes, then that person either becomes angry or feels low, and in the course of their reaction will not be able to manage the situation and may spread negative energy. But an enlightened person will instead show their acceptance of such a situation. He or she will not react instinctively, but instead will accept the problem and try to find an amicable solution, trying to find a way out of that situation or to resolve the issue instead of running away. Enlightenment means you start looking at worldly problems from a higher perspective, you assess them subjectively and act more wisely than the majority of society would. Your understanding of the problem is deeper as you visualise a future that is still decades or even centuries ahead, a place that can provide a more peaceful solution to this world's ills. Enlightened persons will maintain their calm and exude a positive approach to tackling odd situations.

All religions, either directly or indirectly, talk about enlightenment. According to Eastern philosophies (such as Hinduism, Buddhism, or the Tao), once you attain enlightenment through an arduous path of meditation and good karma, you become free from the cycle of birth and rebirth and when you die you attain Samadhi. This means that you now have the freedom to choose whether you want to undergo another birth or not. If you choose to accept another birth you can plan it accordingly – get born and finish your objective – then leave this world. In order for an enlightened person to be reborn in this world, they should have a strong sense of purpose to do something important for humanity and the world. Enlightenment gives you the freedom to become the master of your birth–rebirth process.

In the same manner, in the context of karma, life, death and universal existence, you always receive what you give. Hence, if your journey moves towards attaining wisdom, living a life with good karma and becoming wiser with each passing day, and finally becoming a self-realised (enlightened) person, then your death should happen with complete awareness – and then you break the chain of birth–rebirth and you become master of your own soul. This is what Samadhi or enlightenment means.

Enlightenment does not happen after death; it always happens when you are in your body and alive, as your soul requires a body to attain self-realisation. That is why there is a great importance attached to both body and soul, and you cannot imagine one without the other. For example, a tongue on its own is not enough, as you need food to taste with it and food on its own is not enough, as you need a tongue to taste it with.

There is no specific age at which enlightenment occurs, it could happen at any age and it might also be possible that you were born as an enlightened human with the specific purpose to spread a message of peace and love. But it is more likely that you were born as an average person and while living in this world, via previous karma, you became enlightened through a sheer passion for the truth and learned through a deep understanding of life. There are so many different ways to achieve enlightenment, and it is difficult to say which path is better.

Once you become enlightened, your words and actions make more sense and you become a beacon for the present and coming generations. You become compassionate and loving, and show your kindness towards all living beings without any judgement.

The inward journey towards enlightenment is somewhat similar to the outside world's technical advancement that is also never-ending. What looks advanced today in the technological world will be treated as outdated tomorrow, just like your phones and electronic devices that keep getting updated every few months. But if you start to evolve from the inside, where your soul starts becoming rich as you advance deeper, it never becomes obsolete. It lasts forever. The advancement of the soul is a never-ending process, but once you start moving up, you never go down. You keep growing as your consciousness advances. The more aware you become from the inside, the more beautiful your behaviour, character, and also this world becomes, because the outside world is a reflection of the inside world. Our focus, therefore, is on the advancement of the soul and the move towards enlightenment.

But how can one move towards enlightenment?

If you want an object to levitate, you have to move

it away from the force of gravity. The gravitational force will be reduced the more you move away from the Earth's surface. In the same manner, the more you become detached from earthly things (money, power, physical attachments, fame, greed, ego, violence, and lust), the more you will be able to experience the higher things that exist in this universe and the more elevated you will become in the spiritual world. But the practice of detachment will not happen suddenly, so you need to practise this every day and slowly, slowly you will meet the objective.

The purpose of human life is to attain enlightenment while living in this world and to die with complete awareness, so that you become master of your soul and can break away from the circle of birth–rebirth.

Therefore enlightenment is a beautiful journey but, even once you achieve it, you live like a normal person, and the only difference is that you start contributing towards society in a non-violent, creative, peaceful, and loving way. You start bringing the world together and showing the light to millions around the world. Your life in itself becomes a teaching and you live only for others in a selfless manner, like Krishna, Mahatma Buddha, or Jesus Christ.

SHANTIH SUTRA 21

Who Am I?

First stage
Breathe in and out 30 times with closed eyes, and then wait for one minute.

Breathe in and out 30 times with closed eyes, and then wait for one minute and move to the second stage.

Second stage: 10 minutes
Sit silently with closed eyes for 10 minutes, and then proceed to the next stage.

Third stage: 25 minutes
With your eyes still closed, say the words 'Who am I?'

non-stop for 10 minutes. While doing this, you have to press more emphasis on the 'who'. So when you say 'who', say it deeply. Do not rush when asking this question, but keep saying it slowly and with the defined purpose that you are trying to know yourself and who you really are. What is the real purpose of your existence? After 10 minutes, take a break of 5 minutes and then repeat the same exercise for another 10 minutes.

Fourth stage: 10 minutes
Now lie down on the floor with closed eyes and observe your body, as if viewing it from above. Experience how your soul is separate from your body.

The word 'who' is spiritually deep and it hits your energy around your navel (Manipur Chakra, or the 3rd chakra), allowing it to come into action. Once the energy hiding behind your navel's chakra becomes active, it helps you to fill yourself with compassion and love. It makes you non-judgemental, and gives you better insight into the world.

The exercise will help you understand who really you are, what is the purpose of your life, and in what direction you should move. We are all lost in life, some for good reasons but most of us for bad reasons, and it is better to discover ourselves before it is too late. This meditation technique will give you the basic direction you seek.

THANK YOU

A big thanks to the readers for going through this book. A big thanks that you spent some time reading these chapters and practising their exercises. As human beings we can only plough the field, sow the seeds and patiently wait for the crops to come. The crops are not in our hand yet – they belong to the future, but the actions that grow and ripen them are completely in the here and now. If you keep practising each day, then there is nothing that can stop you from achieving inner peace and happiness. If your focus is to find peace, then you will achieve it. Whenever we put our whole energy towards achieving something, the universe comes forward in turn to help us. A Chinese proverb summarises my book in a single line – **'I hear and I forget. I see and I remember. I do and I understand.'** So please keep reading all the chapters and doing the exercises many times.

I am also learning each day and my learning is endless – the more I learn the more I become hungry to learn, and this hunger for attaining wisdom is a beautiful journey and I wish the same for every person who exists on this beautiful earth.

It would be great to hear and read the feedback from readers who have gone through this book. Also, if you spot any mistakes, please inform me. It would therefore be a great pleasure if you write your feedback and suggestions to the following email address: chittranjan.dubey@gmail.com

Thanks again!
Love & Peace
Chit

ABOUT THE AUTHOR

Chit Dubey is a meditation teacher and a consultant in the IT industry. In the past decade, he has experienced many different areas of life. At the peak of his corporate career when he was given the opportunity to work in the USA, he quit his job for two years and lived a nomad life within India. He was in search of himself during this phase of his life. Later he tried writing and acting in the Bollywood film industry, but with time he realised this was not what he wanted from life. He then volunteered for four months full-time with an NGO (India Against Corruption) in Mumbai, which was running India's biggest socio-political movement at that time. He organised many protests in Mumbai and handled the social media campaign for the Mumbai team. With this organisation he had an opportunity to work with some nationally known sociopolitical activists, and it helped him to understand the sociopolitical world. Later he moved to the African continent and worked in four different countries, followed by living and working in Spain and the UK. With time he realised that spirituality was the one subject closest to his heart and started teaching meditation and giving lectures on spirituality in Tanzania and the UK.

Chit is well-travelled, has lived in many different countries around the world and through this he learned, unlearned, experienced and decided to share his observations of life through this book.